THE ULT

SERBIAN

PHRASE BOOK

1001 SERBIAN PHRASES FOR BEGINNERS AND BEYOND!

BY ADRIAN GEE

ISBN: 979-8-873303-46-5

Author's Note

Welcome to "The Ultimate Serbian Phrase Book." I am thrilled to guide you on a captivating journey into the depths of Serbian, a language renowned for its expressive richness and cultural depth. Whether you're drawn to the historical majesty of Belgrade, the breathtaking beauty of the Serbian countryside, or captivated by the vibrant traditions and soulful music of Serbia, this book is meticulously designed to make your learning experience as immersive and fulfilling as possible.

As a passionate linguist and an enthusiastic proponent of cultural immersion, I recognize the intricate process of mastering a new language. This book emerges from that recognition, aiming to be your comprehensive guide in your pursuit of Serbian proficiency.

Connect with Me: Language learning is more than just absorbing words and grammar—it's about forming connections, understanding a culture's heart and soul. I warmly invite you to join me and other language enthusiasts on Instagram: @adriangruszka, where we foster a community of knowledge sharing and vibrant experiences.

Sharing is Caring: If this book becomes a pivotal part of your language learning journey, I would be deeply honored by your recommendation to others who also value the richness of our world's linguistic diversity. Feel free to share your progress or moments of language victory on Instagram, and don't forget to tag me – I am excited to celebrate your achievements with you!

Embarking on the path to learning Serbian is like exploring a land filled with stories, traditions, and a warm communal essence. Embrace the challenges, rejoice in your progress, and cherish every step of your Serbian adventure.

Srećno! (Good luck!)

- Adrian Gee

CONTENTS

INTRODUCTION

Dobro došli! (Welcome!)

Whether you are enchanted by the vibrant rhythms of a traditional kolo dance, planning to stroll the historic streets of Belgrade, seeking to connect with Serbian speakers, or simply falling in love with the Serbian language for its rich expressiveness, this phrase book is crafted to be your faithful companion.

Embarking on the journey of learning Serbian opens doors to a world characterized by its passionate soul, a storied history, and a commitment to the warmth and resilience reflected in the Serbian spirit.

Zašto srpski? (Why Serbian?)

With its roots deeply embedded in the Slavic language family, Serbian is not only the voice of captivating folk tales and soulful music, but also a critical link in the Balkans for communication, business, and cultural exchange. As an official language in Serbia, Bosnia and Herzegovina, and a recognized minority language in several neighboring countries, Serbian is an invaluable asset for travelers, business professionals, and anyone intrigued by its captivating charm.

Izgovor (Pronunciation)

Before we dive into the rich tapestry of phrases and expressions, it's vital to acquaint yourself with the rhythmic heart of Serbian. Each language has its own melody, and Serbian resonates with a vigor that is both deep and lively, echoing the spirit of its people and landscapes. While mastering its pronunciation might appear challenging initially, with consistent practice, the emphatic tones and melodious cadence of Serbian will become an exhilarating part of your language journey.

Serbian pronunciation is marked by its robust, clear vowel sounds and the distinctive roll of the 'r's. The language's rhythm and stress patterns, along with its unique set of sounds, set it apart from other languages. Perfecting your pronunciation not only aids in clear communication but also deepens your connection with the rich heritage and heart of the Serbian people.

Srpska Azbuka (The Serbian Alphabet)

The Serbian alphabet is a variant of the Cyrillic script and consists of 30 letters. Each letter corresponds to one sound, making Serbian highly phonetic. This makes pronunciation straightforward once you are familiar with the sounds each letter represents.

Vokali (Vowels)

A (a): Like the "a" in "father."
E (e): Like the "e" in "bet."
I (и): Similar to the "ee" in "see."
O (o): Like the "o" in "port," but shorter.
U (y): Similar to the "oo" in "food."

Konsonanti (Consonants)

B (б): As in English "bat."
V (в): Like the "v" in "victory."
G (г): Like the "g" in "go."
D (д): Like the "d" in "dog."
Đ (ђ): Similar to the "j" in "juice."
Z (з): Like the "z" in "zebra."
Ž (ж): Similar to the "s" in "pleasure."
Dž (џ): Similar to the "j" in "jump."
K (к): Like the "k" in "kite."
L (л): As in English "love."

Lj (љ): Similar to the "lli" in "million."
M (м): Like the English "m" in "mother."
N (н): Like the "n" in "nice."
Nj (њ): Like the "ni" in "onion."
P (п): As in English "pen."
R (р): A rolling "r," pronounced at the front of the mouth.
S (с): Like the "s" in "see."
T (т): Like the "t" in "top."
F (ф): As in English "far."
H (x): Similar to the "h" in "hello."
C (ц): Like the "ts" in "cats."
Č (ч): Similar to the "ch" in "check."
Š (ш): Like the "sh" in "shell."

The unique letters:

Ć (ħ): Similar to the "ch" in "cheese," but softer.
J (ј): Like the "y" in "yes."

Note that the Serbian alphabet is highly phonemic, meaning each letter consistently represents the same sound. This makes pronunciation more intuitive than in many other languages. Familiarizing yourself with these sounds is a key step in mastering Serbian pronunciation.

Serbian Intonation and Stress Patterns

Serbian intonation is characterized by its expressiveness, a feature that is central to Slavic languages. Generally, stress in Serbian words can fall on any syllable, and it's crucial to listen for this as it can change the meaning of words.

Common Pronunciation Challenges

Izazovi u Izgovoru (Challenges in Pronunciation)

The Serbian language hosts a variety of sounds, some of which might be unfamiliar to English speakers. Mastering these, especially the unique consonant formations like 'č', 'ć', 'đ', and 'ž', is crucial.

Tips for Practicing Pronunciation

1. **Pažljivo Slušajte (Listen Carefully):** Listening to Serbian music, podcasts, and watching Serbian films or TV shows is a great way to become accustomed to the nuances of the language.

2. **Ponavljajte za Izvornim Govornikom (Repeat After a Native Speaker):** Engaging with a native Serbian speaker, whether in person or through language learning apps, is invaluable for refining your pronunciation.

3. **Koristite Ogledalo (Use a Mirror):** Watching your mouth movements can help in making sure your articulation of Serbian sounds is correct.

4. **Redovno Vežbajte (Practice Regularly):** Consistent practice, even for a few minutes daily, is key to improving.

5. **Ne Bojte se Grešaka (Don't Fear Mistakes):** Embrace errors as they are a crucial part of learning and lead to greater understanding and proficiency.

Clear pronunciation is fundamental in embracing the rich sounds of Serbian. Dedicate yourself to mastering the unique consonants and the melodic intonation, and you'll find the language unfolding like a vivid tapestry. From the robust roll of the 'r's to the softness of 'lj' and 'nj' sounds, each nuance captures the essence of Serbia's storied history and culture.

What You'll Find Inside

- **Bitne Fraze (Essential Phrases):** A carefully curated collection of phrases and expressions for various situations you may encounter in Serbian-speaking environments.

- **Interaktivne Vežbe (Interactive Exercises):** Engaging exercises designed to test and enhance your language skills, encouraging active use of Serbian.

- **Kulturni Uvidi (Cultural Insights):** Delve into the rich culture of Serbian-speaking regions, from their social customs to historical landmarks.

- **Dodatni Resursi (Additional Resources):** A guide to further materials and advice for deepening your understanding of the Serbian language, including websites, literature recommendations, and travel tips.

How to Use This Phrase Book

This book is thoughtfully designed for both beginners embarking on their initial exploration of Serbian and intermediate learners looking to refine their skills. Begin your language journey with essential phrases perfect for a variety of situations, from simple greetings to navigating the subtleties of Serbian social norms. As you gain confidence, progress to more intricate language patterns and idiomatic expressions that bring you closer to the fluency of a native speaker.

Within these pages, you'll find cultural insights that deepen your connection with Serbia's rich history and its vibrant present. Interactive exercises are strategically interspersed to reinforce your learning and help you seamlessly incorporate new vocabulary and grammar into your conversations.

Learning a language is more than just memorizing words and rules—it's an exciting, continuous pursuit of understanding and connection. Dive into Serbian dialogues, explore the country's renowned literary treasures, and engage with traditions that are woven into the fabric of this unique culture.

Each person's journey to language proficiency is unique, characterized by its own rhythm and achievements. Nurture your skills with dedication, passion, and a sense of exploration. With consistent effort, your competence and confidence in Serbian will not just grow; they will flourish.

Spremni za početak? (Ready to start?)

Embark on a captivating journey into the heart of the Serbian language and culture. Uncover the intricacies of its linguistic charm and immerse yourself in the cultural richness that Serbia offers. This adventure is as enriching as it is transformative, expanding your horizons and strengthening your global connections.

GREETINGS & INTRODUCTIONS

- BASIC GREETINGS -
- INTRODUCING YOURSELF AND OTHERS -
- EXPRESSING POLITENESS AND FORMALITY -

Basic Greetings

1. Hi!
   Ћао!
   (Chow!)

2. Hello!
   Здраво!
   (Zdrah-vo!)

> **Idiomatic Expression:** "Бити на седмом небу." -
> Meaning: "To be extremely happy."
> (Literal Translation: "To be on the seventh heaven.")

3. Good morning!
   Добро јутро!
   (Doh-broh yoo-troh!)

> **Cultural Insight:** Serbian hospitality is legendary, with
> guests often treated like family members.

4. Good afternoon!
   Добар дан!
   (Doh-bar dan!)

5. Good evening!
   Добро вече!
   (Doh-broh veh-cheh!)

6. How are you?
   Како си?
   (Kah-koh see?)

   > **Cultural Insight:** Serbians take great pride in their
   > language and its history, often engaging in discussions
   > about its nuances.

7. Everything good?
   Све добро?
   (Sveh doh-broh?)

8. How is it going?
   Како иде?
   (Kah-koh ee-deh?)

9. How is everything?
   Како је све?
   (Kah-koh yeh sveh?)

10. I'm good, thank you.
    Добро сам, хвала.
    (Doh-broh sahm, hva-lah.)

11. And you?
    А ти?
    (Ah tee?)

12. Let me introduce...
    Дозволите да представим...
    (Doz-voh-lee-teh dah prehd-stah-veem...)

13. This is...
    Ово је...
    (O-voh yeh...)

14. Nice to meet you!
    Драго ми је да се упознамо!
    (Drah-go mee yeh dah seh oo-pohz-nah-moh!)

15. Delighted!
    Очаран сам/очарана сам!
    (O-char-an sahm/o-char-ah-nah sahm!)

16. How have you been?
    Како сте? / Како си?
    (Kah-koh steh?) / (Kah-koh see?)

Politeness and Formality

17. Excuse me.
    Извините.
    (Eez-vee-nee-teh.)

18. Please.
    Молим.
    (Moh-leem.)

19. Thank you.
    Хвала.
    (Hvah-lah.)

> **Fun Fact:** Over 17 Roman Emperors were born in the territory of modern-day Serbia.

20. Thank you very much!
    Много хвала!
    (Mnoh-goh hvah-lah!)

21. I'm sorry.
    Жао ми је.
    (Zhao mee yeh.)

22. I apologize.
    Извињавам се.
    (Eez-veen-yah-vahm seh.)

23. Sir
    Господине
    (Gohs-poh-dee-neh)

24. Madam
    Госпођо
    (Gohs-poh-djoh)

25. Miss
    Госпођице
    (Gohs-poh-djee-tseh)

26. Your name, please?
    Како се зовете?
    (Kah-koh seh zoh-veh-teh?)

27. Can I help you with anything?
    Могу ли Вам помоћи нечим?
    (Moh-goo lee vahm poh-moh-chee neh-cheem?)

28. I am thankful for your help.
    Захвалан сам на вашој помоћи.
    (Zah-vah-lahn sahm nah vah-shoy poh-moh-chee.)

29. The pleasure is mine.
    Задовољство је моје.
    (Zah-doh-vohl-stvo yeh moy-yeh.)

30. Thank you for your hospitality.
    Хвала на гостопримству.
    (Hvah-lah nah goh-stoh-preem-stvoo.)

31. It's nice to see you again.
    Драго ми је да вас поново видим.
    (Drah-goh mee yeh dah vahs poh-noh-voh vee-deem.)

Greetings for Different Time of Day

32. Good morning, my friend!
    Добро јутро, пријатељу!
    (Doh-broh yoo-troh, pree-ya-teh-lyoo!)

33. Good afternoon, colleague!
    Добар дан, колега!
    (Doh-bar dan, koh-leh-gah!)

34. Good evening neighbor!
    Добро вече, комшијо!
    (Doh-broh veh-cheh, kohm-shee-yoh!)

35. Have a good night!
    Лаку ноћ!
    (Lah-koo nohch!)

36. Sleep well!
    Спавај добро!
    (Spah-vahy doh-broh!)

Special Occasions

37. Happy birthday!
    Срећан рођендан!
    (Sreh-chan roh-jen-dahn!)

> **Language Learning Tip:** Learn Cyrillic Script -
> Familiarize yourself with the Cyrillic alphabet used in
> Serbian.

38. Merry Christmas!
    Срећан Божић!
    (Sreh-chan Boh-zheech!)

39. Happy Easter!
    Срећан Ускрс!
    (Sreh-chan Oo-skrs!)

> **Travel Story:** In the bustling Zeleni Venac market in
> Belgrade, a vendor described a rare antique with, "Наћи
> иглу у пласту сена," which translates to "Finding a
> needle in a haystack," highlighting a rare find.

40. Happy holidays!
    Срећни празници!
    (Sreh-chnee prahz-nee-tsee!)

41. Happy New Year!
    Срећна Нова Година!
    (Sreh-ch-nah No-vah Goh-dee-nah!)

> **Idiomatic Expression:** "Као мачку око репа." -
> Meaning: "To talk in circles."
> (Literal Translation: "Like a cat around its tail.")

Meeting Someone for the First Time

42. Pleasure to meet you.
    Драго ми је да се упознајемо.
    (Drah-go mee yeh dah seh oo-pohz-nah-yeh-moh.)

> **Language Learning Tip:** Label Household Items - Put labels on everyday items in your home with their Serbian names.

43. I am [Your Name].
    Зовем се [Your Name].
    (Zoh-vehm seh [Your Name].)

44. Where are you from?
    Одакле сте?
    (Oh-dah-kleh steh?)

> **Language Learning Tip:** Keep a Vocabulary Journal - Write down new words and phrases you learn.

45. I'm on vacation.
    На одмору сам.
    (Nah ohd-moh-roo sahm.)

46. What is your profession?
    Које је ваше занимање?
    (Koh-yeh yeh vah-sheh zah-nee-mah-nyeh?)

47. How long will you stay here?
    Колико дуго ћете остати овде?
    (Koh-lee-koh doo-goh chyeh-teh oh-stah-tee ohv-deh?)

Responding to Greetings

48. Hello, how have you been?
    Здраво, како си?
    (Zdrah-vo, kah-koh see?)

> **Cultural Insight:** Coffee, especially Turkish-style, is a crucial part of daily life, symbolizing leisure and conversation.

49. I've been very busy lately.
    У последње време сам био веома заузет.
    (Oo poh-sled-nyeh vreh-meh sahm bee-oh veh-oh-mah zah-oo-zet.)

50. I've had ups and downs.
    Имало је успона и падова.
    (Ee-mah-loh yeh oos-poh-nah ee pah-doh-vah.)

> **Idiomatic Expression:** "Бацити око." -
> Meaning: "To take a look."
> Literal Translation: "To throw an eye."

51. Thanks for asking.
    Хвала што сте питали.
    (Hvah-lah shtoh steh pee-tah-lee.)

52. I feel great.
   Осећам се одлично.
   (Oh-seh-cham seh ohd-leech-noh.)

53. Life has been good.
   Живот је био добар.
   (Zhee-vot yeh bee-oh doh-bar.)

54. I can't complain.
   Не могу да се жалим.
   (Neh moh-goo dah seh zhah-leem.)

55. And you, how are you?
   А ти, како си?
   (Ah tee, kah-koh see?)

   Language Learning Tip: Use Flashcards - Create flashcards for vocabulary and common phrases.

56. I've had some challenges.
   Имао/имала сам изазова.
   (Ee-mah-oh/ee-mah-lah sahm ee-zah-zoh-vah.)

57. Life is a journey.
   Живот је путовање.
   (Zhee-vot yeh poo-toh-vah-nyeh.)

58. Thank God, I'm fine.
   Хвала Богу, добро сам.
   (Hvah-lah Boh-goo, doh-broh sahm.)

Informal Greetings

59. What's up?
 Шта има ново?
 (Shta ee-mah noh-voh?)

60. All good?
 Све у реду?
 (Sveh oo reh-doo?)

61. Hi, everything okay?
 Ћао, све у реду?
 (Chow, sve oo reh-doo?)

62. I'm good, and you?
 Добро сам, а ти?
 (Doh-broh sahm, ah tee?)

63. How's life?
 Како је живот?
 (Kah-koh yeh zhee-vot?)

64. Cool!
 Одлично!
 (Ohd-leech-noh!)

Saying Goodbye

65. Goodbye!
 Довиђења!
 (Doh-vee-jen-ya!)

66. See you later!
Видимо се касније!
(Vee-dee-moh seh kahs-nee-yeh!)

> **Language Learning Tip:** Listen to Serbian Music - Helps in getting used to the rhythm and sound of the language.

67. Bye!
Ћао!
(Chow!)

68. Have a good day.
Леп дан.
(Lep dahn.)

> **Language Learning Tip:** Watch Serbian TV Shows and Movies - Enhances listening skills and cultural understanding.

69. Have a good weekend.
Леп викенд.
(Lep vee-kend.)

70. Take care.
Чувај се.
(Choo-vahy seh.)

71. Bye, see you later.
Ћао, видимо се касније.
(Chow, vee-dee-moh seh kahs-nee-yeh.)

72. I need to go now.
Морам сада да идем.
(Moh-rahm sah-dah dah ee-dehm.)

73. Take care my friend!
   Чувај се, пријатељу!
   (Choo-vahy seh, pree-ya-teh-lyoo!)

Parting Words

74. Hope to see you soon.
   Надам се да ћемо се ускоро видети.
   (Nah-dahm seh dah cheh-moh seh oos-koh-roh vee-deh-tee.)

75. Stay in touch.
   Останите у контакту.
   (Ohs-tah-nee-teh oo kohn-tahk-too.)

76. I'll miss you.
   Недостајаћеш ми.
   (Neh-doh-stah-yah-chesh mee.)

77. Be well.
   Буди добро.
   (Boo-dee doh-broh.)

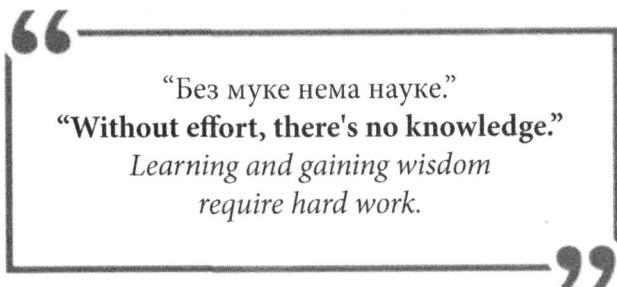

> "Без муке нема науке."
> **"Without effort, there's no knowledge."**
> *Learning and gaining wisdom*
> *require hard work.*

Interactive Challenge: Greetings Quiz

1. **How do you say "good morning" in Serbian?**

   a) Шта радиш?
   b) Добро јутро!
   c) Како си?

2. **What does the Serbian phrase "Драго ми је што смо се упознали" mean in English?**

   a) Excuse me!
   b) Pleased to meet you!
   c) How are you?

3. **When is it appropriate to use the phrase "Добро вече!" in Serbian?**

   a) In the morning
   b) In the afternoon
   c) In the evening

4. **Which phrase is used to ask someone how they are doing in Serbian?**

   a) Хвала
   b) Како си?
   c) Где идеш?

5. **In Serbia, when can you use the greeting "Здраво!"?**

   a) Only in the morning
   b) Only in the afternoon
   c) Anytime

6. What is the Serbian equivalent of "And you?"?

    a) А ти?
    b) Хвала
    c) Шта радиш?

7. When expressing gratitude in Serbian, what do you say?

    a) Извините
    b) Драго ми је што смо се упознали
    c) Хвала

8. How do you say "Excuse me" in Serbian?

    a) Извините
    b) Добар дан!
    c) Све у реду?

9. Which phrase is used to inquire about someone's well-being?

    a) Где живиш?
    b) Како си?
    c) Хвала

10. In a typical Serbian conversation, when is it common to ask about someone's background and interests during a first-time meeting?

    a) Never
    b) Only in formal situations
    c) Always

11. In Serbian, what does "Драго ми је што смо се упознали" mean?

a) Delighted to meet you
b) Excuse me
c) Thank you

12. When should you use the phrase "Како си?"?

a) When ordering food
b) When asking for directions
c) When inquiring about someone's well-being

13. Which phrase is used to make requests politely?

a) Како си?
b) Шта желиш?
c) Молим

14. What is the equivalent of "I'm sorry" in Serbian?

a) Жао ми је
b) Како си?
c) Све је у реду

Correct Answers:

1. b)
2. b)
3. c)
4. b)
5. c)
6. a)
7. c)
8. a)
9. b)
10. c)
11. a)
12. c)
13. c)
14. a)

EATING & DINING

- ORDERING FOOD AND DRINKS IN A RESTAURANT -
- DIETARY PREFERENCES AND RESTRICTIONS -
- COMPLIMENTS AND COMPLAINTS ABOUT FOOD -

Basic Ordering

78. I'd like a table for two, please.
    Желео/Желела бих сто за двоје, молим.
    (Zheh-leh-oh/Zheh-leh-lah beeh stoh zah dvo-yeh, moh-leem.)

79. What's the special of the day?
    Које је данашње специјално јело?
    (Koh-yeh yeh dah-nahsh-nyeh speh-tsee-yahl-noh yeh-loh?)

> **Cultural Insight:** Traditional Serbian taverns (kafanas) are central social hubs where people gather to eat, drink, and enjoy music.

80. Can I see the menu, please?
    Могу ли да видим мени, молим?
    (Moh-goo lee dah vee-deem meh-nee, moh-leem?)

81. I'll have the steak, medium rare.
    Узећу бифтек, средње печен.
    (Oo-ze-chu beef-tek, srehd-nyeh peh-chen.)

82. Can I get a glass of water?
    Могу ли добити чашу воде, молим?
    (Moh-goo lee doh-bee-tee chah-shoo voh-deh, moh-leem?)

> **Travel Story:** While exploring the ancient Niš Fortress, a guide used the phrase, "Старији од памети," meaning "Older than memory," to describe its historical significance.

83. Can you bring us some bread to start?
Можете ли нам донети хлеб за почетак?
(Moh-zheh-teh lee nahm doh-neh-tee khleb zah poh-cheh-tahk?)

84. Do you have a vegetarian option?
Имате ли вегетаријанску опцију?
(Ee-mah-teh lee veh-geh-tah-ree-yan-skoo op-tsee-yoo?)

> **Language Learning Tip:** Record Yourself Speaking -
> Helps in self-assessment and pronunciation
> improvement.

85. Is there a kids' menu available?
Имате ли дечији мени?
(Ee-mah-teh lee deh-chee-yee meh-nee?)

86. We'd like to order appetizers to share.
Желели бисмо да наручимо предјела за дељење.
(Zheh-leh-lee bees-moh dah nah-roo-chee-moh preh-dye-lah zah deh-lyeh-nyeh.)

87. Can we have separate checks, please?
Можемо ли добити посебне рачуне, молим?
(Moh-zheh-moh lee doh-bee-tee poh-sehb-neh rah-choo-neh, moh-leem?)

88. Could you recommend a vegetarian dish?
Можете ли препоручити вегетаријанско јело?
(Moh-zheh-teh lee preh-poh-roo-chee-tee veh-geh-tah-ree-yan-skoh yeh-loh?)

89. I'd like to try the local cuisine.
Желео/Желела бих да пробам локалну кухињу.
(Zheh-leh-oh/Zheh-leh-lah beeh dah proh-bahm loh-kahl-noo koo-heen-yoo.)

90. May I have a refill on my drink, please?
Може ли да ми напуните пиће поново, молим?
(Moh-zheh lee dah mee nah-poo-nee-teh pee-tcheh poh-noh-voh, moh-leem?)

91. What's the chef's special today?
Какав је данашњи специјалитет кувара?
(Kah-kahv yeh dah-nahsh-nyee speh-tsee-yah-lee-teht koo-vah-rah?)

92. Can you make it extra spicy?
Можете ли га направити љућим, молим?
(Moh-zheh-teh lee gah nah-prah-vee-tee lyoo-cheem, moh-leem?)

93. I'll have the chef's tasting menu.
Узећу дегустациони мени кувара.
(Oo-ze-choo deh-goo-stah-tsee-oh-nee meh-nee koo-vah-rah.)

Special Requests

94. I'm allergic to nuts. Is this dish nut-free?
Алергичан/алергична сам на орашасто. Да ли је ово јело без орашастих?
(Ah-lehr-gee-chan/ah-lehr-gee-ch-nah sahm nah oh-rah-shah-stoh. Dah lee yeh oh-voh yeh-loh behz oh-rah-shahs-tee?)

95. I'm on a gluten-free diet. What can I have?
На безглутенској дијети сам. Шта могу да наручим?
(Nah behz-gloo-ten-skoy dee-yeh-tee sahm. Shta moh-goo dah nah-roo-cheem?)

96. Can you make it less spicy, please?
Можете ли га направити мање љуто, молим?
(Moh-zheh-teh lee gah nah-prah-vee-tee mah-nyeh lyoo-toh, moh-leem?)

> **Idiomatic Expression:** "Златна средина." -
> Meaning: "A happy medium."
> (Literal translation: "The golden middle.")

97. Can you recommend a local specialty?
Можете ли препоручити локални специјалитет?
(Moh-zheh-teh lee preh-poh-roo-chee-tee loh-kahl-nee speh-tsee-yah-lee-teht?)

98. Could I have my salad without onions?
Могу ли добити салату без лука?
(Moh-goo lee doh-bee-tee sah-lah-too behz loo-kah?)

99. Are there any daily specials?
Имате ли данашње специјалитете?
(Ee-mah-teh lee dah-nahsh-nyeh speh-tsee-yah-lee-teh-teh?)

> **Fun Fact:** Europe's second-longest river, the Danube, flows through Serbia.

> "Лакше је обећати него испунити."
> **"It's easier to promise than to fulfill."**
> *Committing to something is easy, but following through can be difficult.*

100. Can I get a side of extra sauce?
      Могу ли добити мало додатног соса?
      (Moh-goo lee doh-bee-tee mah-loh doh-daht-nog soh-sah?)

101. I'd like a glass of red/white wine, please.
      Молим вас, једну чашу црвеног/белог вина.
      *(Moh-leem vahs, yehd-noo chah-shoo tsr-veh-nog/be-lohg
      vee-nah.)*

102. Could you bring the bill, please?
      Можете ли ми донети рачун, молим?
      (Moh-zheh-teh lee mee doh-neh-tee rah-choon, moh-leem?)

Allergies and Intolerances

103. I have a dairy allergy. Is the sauce dairy-free?
      **Алергичан/алергична сам на млечне производе. Да ли је
      сос без млека?**
      *(Ah-lehr-gee-chan/ah-lehr-gee-ch-nah sahm nah mlehch-neh
      pro-eez-voh-deh. Dah lee yeh sohs behz mleh-kah?)*

104. Does this contain any seafood? I have an allergy.
      **Да ли ово садржи морске производе? Алергичан/
      алергична сам.**
      *(Dah lee oh-voh sah-dzhee mohr-skeh pro-eez-voh-deh?
      Ah-lehr-gee-chan/ah-lehr-gee-ch-nah sahm.)*

105. I can't eat anything with soy. Is that an issue?
      Не могу да једем ништа са сојом. Да ли је то проблем?
      *(Neh moh-goo dah yeh-dehm nee-shtah sah soh-yohm. Dah lee
      yeh toh proh-blem?)*

106. I'm lactose intolerant, so no dairy, please.
Интолерантан/интолерантна сам на лактозу, молим без млечних производа.
(Een-toh-leh-rahn-tahn/een-toh-leh-rahn-tah sahm nah lah-ktoh-zoo, moh-leem behz mlehch-nee pro-eez-voh-dah.)

107. Is there an option for those with nut allergies?
Има ли опција за особе алергичне на орашасте?
(Ee-mah lee op-tsee-yah zah oh-soh-beh ah-lehr-gee-chneh nah oh-rah-shahs-teh?)

108. I'm following a vegan diet. Is that possible?
На веганској дијети сам. Да ли је то могуће?
(Nah veh-gahn-skoy dee-yeh-tee sahm. Dah lee yeh toh moh-goo-cheh?)

> **Fun Fact:** The Serbian town of Vranje is known for having more clocks than residents.

109. Is this dish suitable for someone with allergies?
Да ли је ово јело погодно за особе са алергијама?
(Dah lee yeh oh-voh yeh-loh poh-gohd-noh zah oh-soh-beh sah ah-lehr-gee-ya-mah?)

110. I'm trying to avoid dairy. Any dairy-free options?
Трудим се да избегавам млечне производе. Има ли опција без млека?
(Troo-deem seh dah eez-beh-gah-vahm mlehch-neh pro-eez-voh-deh. Ee-mah lee op-tsee-yah behz mleh-kah?)

111. I have a shellfish allergy. Is it safe to order seafood?
Алергичан/алергична сам на шкољке. Да ли је безбедно наручити морске производе?
(Ah-lehr-gee-chan/ah-lehr-gee-ch-nah sahm nah shkoh-lykeh. Dah lee yeh behz-behd-noh nah-roo-chee-tee mohr-skeh pro-eez-voh-deh?)

112.   Can you make this gluten-free?
   Можете ли ово припремити без глутена?
   (Moh-zheh-teh lee oh-voh pree-preh-mee-tee behz gloo-teh-nah?)

> **Language Learning Tip:** Listen to Serbian Radio - It's a
> good way to immerse yourself in the language.

Specific Dietary Requests

113.   I prefer my food without cilantro.
   Више волим храну без коријандера.
   (Vee-sheh voh-leem khrah-noo behz koh-ree-yan-deh-rah.)

114.   Could I have the dressing on the side?
   Може ли дресинг да буде посебно?
   (Moh-zheh lee dreh-seeng dah boo-deh poh-sehb-noh?)

115.   Can you make it vegan-friendly?
   Можете ли ово припремити вегански?
   (Moh-zheh-teh lee oh-voh pree-preh-mee-tee veh-gahn-skee?)

116.   I'd like extra vegetables with my main course.
   Желео/Желела бих додатно поврће уз главно јело.
   (Zheh-leh-oh/Zheh-leh-lah beeh doh-daht-noh poh-vryeh ooz glahv-noh yeh-loh.)

117.   Is this suitable for someone on a keto diet?
   Да ли је ово погодно за некога на кето дијети?
   (Dah lee yeh oh-voh poh-gohd-noh zah neh-koh-gah nah keh-toh dee-yeh-tee?)

118. I prefer my food with less oil, please.
Више волим храну са мање уља, молим.
(Vee-sheh voh-leem khrah-noo sah mah-nyeh ool-yah, moh-leem.)

119. Is this dish suitable for vegetarians?
Да ли је ово јело погодно за вегетаријанце?
(Dah lee yeh oh-voh yeh-loh poh-gohd-noh zah veh-geh-tah-ree-yan-tseh?)

120. I'm on a low-carb diet. What would you recommend?
На исхрани сам са мало угљених хидрата. Шта бисте препоручили?
(Nah eesh-rah-nee sahm sah mah-loh oogl-yeh-nee-h hee-drah-tah. Shta bees-teh preh-poh-roo-chee-lee?)

> **Fun Fact:** Every letter in the Serbian alphabet corresponds to a unique sound.

121. Is the bread here gluten-free?
Да ли је хлеб овде без глутена?
(Dah lee yeh khleb ohv-deh behz gloo-teh-nah?)

122. I'm watching my sugar intake. Any sugar-free desserts?
Пазим на унос шећера. Има ли безшећерних десерта?
(Pah-zeem nah oo-nos sheh-cheh-rah. Ee-mah lee behz-sheh-chehr-nee-h deh-sehr-tah?)

> **Travel Story:** On the streets of Novi Sad during the famous EXIT Festival, a reveler exclaimed, "Ово је права журка!" meaning "This is a real party!" capturing the vibrant atmosphere.

Compliments

123. This meal is delicious!
Ово јело је укусно!
(Oh-voh yeh-loh yeh oo-koo-snoh!)

> **Fun Fact:** The capital city, Belgrade, is over 7,000 years old.

124. The flavors in this dish are amazing.
Укуси у овом јелу су неверватни.
(Oo-koo-see oo oh-vohm yeh-loo soo neh-veh-roh-vat-nee.)

125. I love the presentation of the food.
Обожавам како је храна послужена.
(Oh-boh-zhah-vahm kah-koh yeh khrah-nah poh-sloo-zheh-nah.)

126. This dessert is outstanding!
Овај десерт је изванредан!
(Oh-vahy deh-sehrt yeh eez-vahn-reh-dahn!)

127. The service here is exceptional.
Услуга овде је изузетна.
(Oo-sloo-gah ohv-deh yeh eez-oo-zeht-nah.)

> **Language Learning Tip:** Set Realistic Goals - Set achievable targets, like learning ten new words a day.

128. The chef deserves praise for this dish.
Кувар заслужује похвалу за ово јело.
(Koo-vahr zah-sloo-zhoo-yeh poh-vah-loo zah oh-voh yeh-loh.)

129. I'm impressed by the quality of the ingredients.
Импресиониран сам квалитетом састојака.
(Eem-preh-see-oh-nee-rahn sahm kvah-lee-teh-tohm sah-stoh-yah-kah.)

130. The atmosphere in this restaurant is wonderful.
Атмосфера у овом ресторану је дивна.
(Aht-mohs-feh-rah oo oh-vohm rehs-toh-rah-noo yeh dee-vnah.)

131. Everything we ordered was perfect.
Све што смо наручили је било савршено.
(Sveh shtoh smoh nah-roo-chee-lee yeh bee-loh sahv-rsheh-noh.)

Compaints

132. The food is cold. Can you reheat it?
Храна је хладна. Можете ли је поново загрејати?
(Khrah-nah yeh khlahd-nah. Moh-zheh-teh lee yeh poh-noh-voh zah-greh-yah-tee?)

> **Fun Fact:** The Kolo, a traditional Serbian dance, is performed in a circle.

133. This dish is too spicy for me.
Ово јело је превише љуто за мене.
(Oh-voh yeh-loh yeh preh-vee-sheh lyoo-toh zah meh-neh.)

134. The portion size is quite small.
Величина порције је прилично мала.
(Veh-lee-chee-nah pohr-tsee-yeh yeh pree-leech-noh mah-lah.)

135. There's a hair in my food.
Има длака у мојој храни.
(Ee-mah dlah-kah oo moh-yoy khrah-nee.)

136. I'm not satisfied with the service.
Нисам задовољан услугом.
(Nee-sahm zah-doh-voh-lyahn oo-sloo-gohm.)

137. The soup is lukewarm.
Супа је млака.
(Soo-pah yeh mlah-kah.)

138. The sauce on this dish is too salty.
Сос на овом јелу је преслан.
(Sohs nah oh-vohm yeh-loo yeh preh-slahn.)

> **Idiomatic Expression:** "Врати се разуму."
> Meaning: "Come back to your senses."
> (Literal translation: "Return to reason.")

139. The dessert was a bit disappointing.
Десерт је био мало разочаравајућ.
(Deh-sehrt yeh bee-oh mah-loh rah-zoh-cha-rah-vah-yooch.)

140. I ordered this dish, but you brought me something else.
Наручио/Наручила сам ово јело, али сте ми донели нешто друго.
(Nah-roo-chee-oh/Nah-roo-chee-lah sahm oh-voh yeh-loh, ah-lee steh mee doh-neh-lee neh-shtoh droo-goh.)

141. The food took a long time to arrive.
Храна је дуго чекала да стигне.
(Khrah-nah yeh doo-goh cheh-kah-lah dah stee-gneh.)

Specific Dish Feedback

142. The steak is overcooked.
Бифтек је препечен.
(Beef-tek yeh preh-peh-chen.)

> **Fun Fact:** Serbian is known for its expressive nature, particularly in poetry and music.

143. This pasta is undercooked.
Ова паста је недовољно кувана.
(Oh-vah pahs-tah yeh neh-doh-voh-lynoh koo-vah-nah.)

144. The fish tastes off. Is it fresh?
Риба има чудан укус. Да ли је свежа?
(Ree-bah ee-mah choo-dahn oo-koos. Dah lee yeh sve-zhah?)

145. The salad dressing is too sweet.
Прелив за салату је пресладак.
(Preh-leev zah sah-lah-too yeh preh-slah-dahk.)

146. The rice is underseasoned.
Пиринач је недовољно зачињен.
(Peer-een-yach yeh neh-doh-voh-lynoh zah-chee-nyehn.)

> **Language Learning Tip:** Subscribe to Serbian YouTube Channels - Find channels that interest you for regular listening practice.

147. The dessert lacks flavor.
Десерту недостаје укус.
(Deh-sehr-too neh-doh-stah-yeh oo-koos.)

148.   The vegetables are overcooked.
        Поврђе је прекувано.
        (Pov-ryeh yeh preh-koo-vah-noh.)

149.   The pizza crust is burnt.
        Кора пице је изгорела.
        (Koh-rah pee-tseh yeh eez-goh-reh-lah.)

> **Travel Story:** At the ethno village of Drvengrad, created by film director Emir Kusturica, a visitor described it as, "Као из бајке," which translates to "Like from a fairy tale."

150.   The burger is dry.
        Бургер је сув.
        (Boor-gher yeh soov.)

151.   The fries are too greasy.
        Помфрит је премасан.
        (Pohm-freet yeh preh-mah-sahn.)

152.   The soup is too watery.
        Супа је превише водена.
        (Soo-pah yeh preh-vee-sheh voh-deh-nah.)

> "Што се мора није тешко."
> **"What must be done is not hard."**
> *Necessity makes difficult tasks easier.*

Word Search Puzzle: Eating & Dining

RESTAURANT
РЕСТОРАН
MENU
МЕНИ
APPETIZER
ПРЕДЈЕЛО
VEGETARIAN
ВЕГЕТАРИЈАНАЦ
ALLERGY
АЛЕРГИЈА
VEGAN
ВЕГАН
SPECIAL
ПОСЕБАН
DESSERT
ДЕСЕРТ
SERVICE
УСЛУГА
CHEF
ГЛАВНИ КУВАР
INGREDIENTS
САСТОЈЦИ
ATMOSPHERE
АТМОСФЕРА
PERFECT
САВРШЕН

```
K M C H V P Y A W R Z L X F M
C P S A O E L E E F K S H H N
Z C Z J C L G S T G V P F A J
D K B G E T T E A R H V T U G
V N Y R D A O U T K V M K F V
P B G W U D E J D A O Z O U A
D Y U R X U G B Ц C R N F Z H
U Y A F T R W R Ф И S I B S Q
K N A J И Г Р Е Л А M P A L B
T Д O L B U P Y R L A K W N E
F E W B L A N E U B J F W U Г
P C O X B I Z E У Y P S L K E
J E Y Q A I S K M L C T Y P T
Q P X Q T П Р Е Д Ј Е Л О A A
Z T A E V T C E F R E P P T P
I T P W C H F V U D H Q C M И
G P Z H R E I E F V A K B O J
A E C E M S D D H U Г S H S A
J F T C H A P O T C E P E P H
A Г У Л С У Д И F O B R G H A
П O C E Б A H H D E V D I E Ц
D Y W O H X Z E M I H U A R W
T E K Q D E L M C S A C A E N
G L S G K A Ш Е И Z N D V D V
A Q U S I R Z P H X F A P M G
U T R C E H X X B W F H G E T
O X E A Q R U L A A R U E E R
R P F G U U T E Л A C K D H V
S Z M V B O O G Г J M G N U S
E V S I N G R E D I E N T S D
```

Correct Answers:

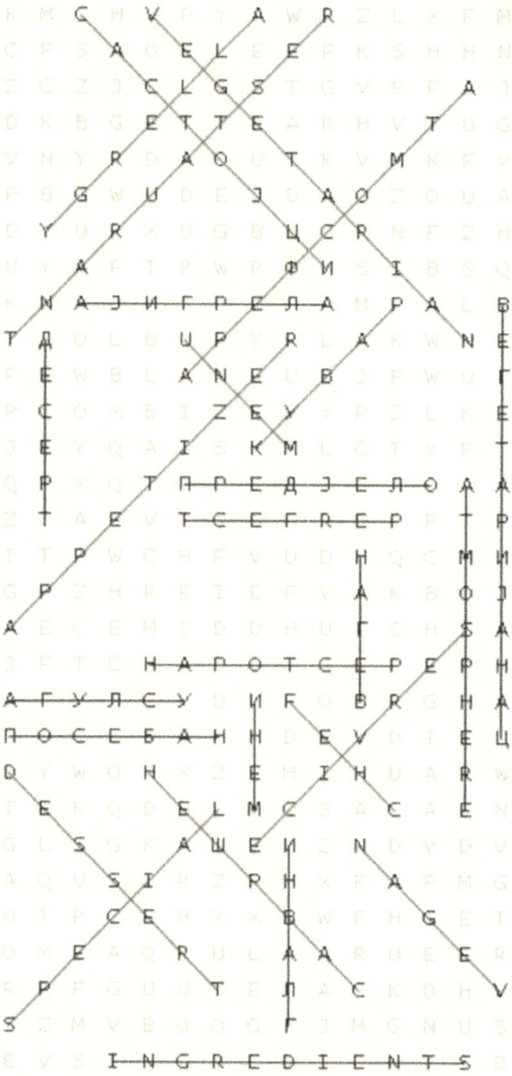

TRAVEL & TRANSPORTATION

- ASKING FOR DIRECTIONS -
- BUYING TICKETS FOR TRANSPORTATION -
- INQUIRING ABOUT TRAVEL-RELATED INFORMATION -

Directions

153.   How do I get to the nearest bus stop?
        Како да стигнем до најближе аутобуске станице?
        *(Kah-koh dah stee-gnem doh nahy-blee-zheh ah-oo-toh-boos-keh
        stah-nee-tseh?)*

> **Fun Fact:** Nikola Tesla, the famous inventor, was of
> Serbian origin.

154.   Can you show me the way to the train station?
        Можете ли ми показати пут до железничке станице?
        *(Moh-zheh-teh lee mee poh-kah-zah-tee poot doh zheh-lez-neech-
        keh stah-nee-tseh?)*

155.   Is there a map of the city center?
        Има ли мапа центра града?
        (Ee-mah lee mah-pah tsehn-trah grah-dah?)

156.   Which street leads to the airport?
        Која улица води до аеродрома?
        (Koh-yah oo-lee-tsah voh-dee doh ah-eh-roh-droh-mah?)

157.   Where is the nearest taxi stand?
        Где је најближи такси стајалиште?
        (Gdeh yeh nahy-blee-zhee tahk-see stah-yah-leesh-teh?)

> **Travel Story:** In a cozy kafana (traditional tavern) in
> Belgrade, locals raised their glasses saying, "Живели!"
> which means "Cheers!" or "To life!"

158. How can I find the hotel from here?
Како могу да нађем хотел одавде?
(Kah-koh moh-goo dah nah-jehm hoh-tehl oh-dahv-deh?)

> **Fun Fact:** Serbia is one of the world's largest producers of raspberries.

159. What's the quickest route to the museum?
Који је најбржи пут до музеја?
(Koh-yee yeh nahy-brzhee poot doh moo-zey-yah?)

160. Is there a pedestrian path to the beach?
Има ли пешачка стаза до плаже?
(Ee-mah lee peh-shach-kah stah-zah doh plah-zheh?)

161. Can you point me towards the city square?
Можете ли ме упутити ка градском тргу?
(Moh-zheh-teh lee meh oo-poo-tee-tee kah grahd-skom trgoo?)

> **Idiomatic Expression:** "Пун као брод." - Meaning: "Very rich."
> (Literal translation: "Full like a ship.")

162. How do I find the trailhead for the hiking trail?
Како да нађем почетак планинарске стазе?
(Kah-koh dah nah-jehm poh-cheh-tahk plah-nee-nar-skeh stah-zeh?)

> **Fun Fact:** Serbia has several UNESCO World Heritage Sites including Studenica Monastery.

Ticket Purchase

163.   How much is a one-way ticket to downtown?
Колико кошта карта у једном правцу до центра?
(Koh-lee-koh koh-shta kahr-tah oo yehd-nom prahv-tsoo doh tsehn-trah?)

164.   Are there any discounts for students?
Има ли попуста за студенте?
(Ee-mah lee poh-poo-stah zah stoo-dehn-teh?)

> **Language Learning Tip:** Attend Serbian Language Workshops or Classes - Structured learning environments can be very beneficial.

165.   What's the price of a monthly bus pass?
Колико кошта месечна аутобуска карта?
(Koh-lee-koh koh-shta meh-sech-nah ah-oo-toh-boos-kah kahr-tah?)

166.   Can I buy a metro ticket for a week?
Могу ли купити седмичну картицу за метро?
(Moh-goo lee koo-pee-tee sed-meech-noo kahr-tee-tsoo zah meh-troh?)

167.   How do I get a refund for a canceled flight?
Како да добијем повраћај новца за отказан лет?
(Kah-koh dah doh-bee-yehm poh-vrah-chahy nohv-tsah zah oht-kah-zahn leht?)

> **Fun Fact:** The Serbian Orthodox Church has a history dating back over 1,200 years.

168. Is it cheaper to purchase tickets online or at the station?
Јефтиније ли је куповати карте онлајн или на станици?
(Yehf-tee-nyeh lee yeh koo-poh-vah-tee kahr-teh ohn-lahyn eely nah stah-nee-tsee?)

169. Can I upgrade my bus ticket to first class?
Могу ли унапредити моју аутобуску карту до прве класе?
(Moh-goo lee oo-nah-preh-dee-tee moh-yoo ah-oo-toh-boos-koo kahr-too doh prveh klah-seh?)

170. Are there any promotions for weekend train travel?
Има ли промоција за викенд путовања возом?
(Ee-mah lee proh-mo-tsee-yah zah vee-kehnd poo-toh-vahn-yah voh-zohm?)

171. Is there a night bus to the city center?
Има ли ноћни аутобус до центра?
(Ee-mah lee nohch-nee ah-oo-toh-boos doh tsehn-trah?)

> **Idiomatic Expression:** "Зелен као паприка." -
> Meaning: "Naive or inexperienced."
> (Literal translation: "Green like a pepper.")

172. What's the cost of a one-day tram pass?
Колико кошта једнодневна трамвајска карта?
(Koh-lee-koh koh-shta yehd-noh-dnev-nah trahm-vahys-kah kahr-tah?)

> **Fun Fact:** Serbian Art and Artists have contributed
> significantly to European art.

Travel Info

173.   What's the weather forecast for tomorrow?
Каква је прогноза за време за сутра?
(Kahk-vah yeh proh-gnoh-zah zah vreh-meh zah soo-trah?)

174.   Are there any guided tours of the historical sites?
Има ли вођених обилазака историјских знаменитости?
(Ee-mah lee voh-jeh-nee-h oh-bee-lah-zah-kah ees-toh-ree-y-skeeh zna-meh-nee-toh-stee?)

175.   Can you recommend a good local restaurant for dinner?
Можете ли препоручити добар локални ресторан за вечеру?
(Moh-zheh-teh lee preh-poh-roo-chee-tee doh-bar loh-kahl-nee rehs-toh-rahn zah veh-cheh-roo?)

176.   How do I get to the famous landmarks in town?
Како да стигнем до познатих знаменитости у граду?
(Kah-koh dah stee-gnem doh pohz-nah-teeh zna-meh-nee-toh-st ee oo grah-doo?)

177.   Is there a visitor center at the airport?
Да ли постоји информациони центар на аеродрому?
(Dah lee poh-stoh-yee een-for-mah-tsee-oh-nee tsehn-tahr nah ah-eh-roh-droh-moo?)

178.   What's the policy for bringing pets on the train?
Каква је политика за ношење кућних љубимаца у возу?
(Kahk-vah yeh poh-lee-tee-kah zah noh-sheh-nyeh kooch-nee-h lyoo-bee-mah-tsah oo voh-zoo?)

179. Are there any discounts for disabled travelers?
Има ли попуста за путнике са инвалидитетом?
(Ee-mah lee poh-poo-stah zah poot-nee-keh sah een-vah-lee-dee-teh-tohm?)

> **Idiomatic Expression:** "Као слон у стаклари." - Meaning: "To be clumsy or awkward in a situation." (Literal translation: "Like an elephant in a glass shop.")

180. Can you provide information about local festivals?
Можете ли дати информације о локалним фестивалима?
(Moh-zheh-teh lee dah-tee een-for-mah-tsee-yeh oh loh-kahl-neem fehs-tee-vah-lee-mah?)

181. Is there Wi-Fi available on long bus journeys?
Да ли постоји Wi-Fi на дугачким аутобуским путовањима?
(Dah lee poh-stoh-yee wee-fee nah doo-gahch-keem ah-oo-toh-boos-keem poo-toh-vahn-yee-mah?)

> **Fun Fact:** Serbia officially uses both Cyrillic and Latin alphabets.

182. Where can I rent a bicycle for exploring the city?
Где могу изнајмити бицикл за обилазак града?
(Gdeh moh-goo eez-nah-y-mee-tee bee-tsee-kl zah oh-bee-lah-zahk grah-dah?)

> **Travel Story:** At the impressive Ђаvolja Varoš (Devil's Town) rock formations, a tourist remarked, "Природа прави најбоље скулптуре," meaning "Nature makes the best sculptures."

Getting Around by Public Transportation

183. Which bus should I take to reach the city center?
Који аутобус треба да узмем да бих дошао/дошла до центра града?
(Koh-yee ah-oo-toh-boos treh-bah dah ooz-mem dah bee-h doh-shah-oh/doh-shlah doh tsehn-trah grah-dah?)

184. Can I buy a day pass for unlimited rides?
Могу ли купити дневну карту за неограничену вожњу?
(Moh-goo lee koo-pee-tee dnehv-noo kahr-too zah neh-oh-grah-nee-cheh-noo vohzhy-oo?)

185. Is there a metro station within walking distance?
Да ли је метро станица на ходној даљини?
(Dah lee yeh meh-troh stah-nee-tsah nah hohd-noy dah-lee-nee?)

186. How do I transfer between different bus lines?
Како да пређем са једне на другу аутобуску линију?
(Kah-koh dah preh-yem sah yehd-neh nah droo-goo ah-oo-toh-boos-koo lee-nee-yoo?)

187. Are there any discounts for senior citizens?
Има ли попуста за старије особе?
(Ee-mah lee poh-poo-stah zah stah-ree-yeh oh-soh-beh?)

188. What's the last bus/train for the night?
Који је последњи аутобус/воз за вече?
(Koh-yee yeh poh-sleh-dnee ah-oo-toh-boos/voz zah veh-cheh?)

189. Are there any express buses to [destination]?
Има ли експресних аутобуса до [дестинације]?
(Ee-mah lee ehk-spreh-sneeh ah-oo-toh-boo-sah doh [deh-stee-nah-tsee-yeh]?)

> "Свака медаља има две стране."
> **"Every medal has two sides."**
> *There are two sides to every story.*

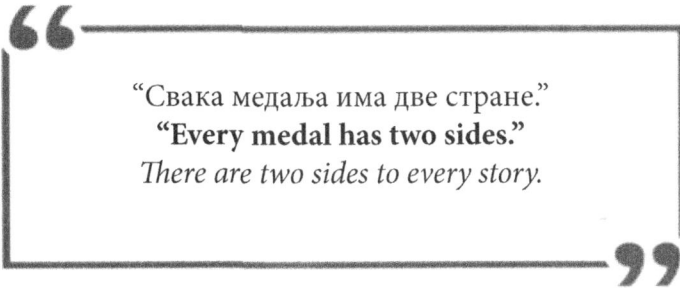

190.　Do trams run on weekends as well?
Да ли трамваји саобраћају и викендом?
(Dah lee trahm-vah-yee sah-oh-brah-chah-yoo ee vee-kehn-dohm?)

> **Fun Fact:** Nis, Serbia, has a tower made from the skulls of Serbian rebels who fought against Ottoman rule.

191.　Can you recommend a reliable taxi service?
Можете ли препоручити поуздану такси услугу?
(Moh-zheh-teh lee preh-poh-roo-chee-tee poh-ooz-dah-noo tahk-see oos-loo-goo?)

192.　What's the fare for a one-way ticket to the suburbs?
Колико кошта карта у једном правцу до предграђа?
(Koh-lee-koh koh-shta kahr-tah oo yehd-nom prahv-tsoo doh prehd-grahd-yah?)

> **Travel Story:** In the peaceful countryside of Vojvodina, a farmer used the saying, "Ко рано рани, две среће граби," meaning "Who rises early, catches two fortunes," reflecting the value of hard work.

Navigating the Airport

193.   Where can I locate the baggage claim area?
Где могу да пронађем простор за преузимање багажа?
*(Gdeh moh-goo dah proh-nah-djem proh-stor zah
preh-oo-zee-mahn-yeh bah-gah-zha?)*

194.   Is there a currency exchange counter in the terminal?
Да ли постоји мењачница у терминалу?
*(Dah lee poh-stoh-yee myen-yahch-nee-tsah oo
tehr-mee-nah-loo?)*

> **Idiomatic Expression:** "Слон у порцелану." -
> Meaning: "To be clumsy."
> (Literal translation: "Elephant in a porcelain shop.")

195.   Are there any pet relief areas for service animals?
Да ли постоје простори за одмор кућних љубимаца?
*(Dah lee poh-stoh-yeh proh-stoh-ree zah oh-dmor kooch-neeh
lyoo-bee-mah-tsah?)*

196.   How early can I go through security?
Колико рано могу проћи кроз безбедност?
(Koh-lee-koh rah-noh moh-goo proh-chee krohz behz-behd-nost?)

197.   What's the procedure for boarding the aircraft?
Какав је поступак за укрцавање у авион?
*(Kah-kahv yeh poh-stoo-pak zah oo-kr-tsah-vahn-yeh oo
ah-vee-ohn?)*

198.   Can I use mobile boarding passes?
Могу ли користити мобилне карте за укрцавање?
*(Moh-goo lee koh-rees-tee-tee moh-beel-neh kahr-teh zah
oo-kr-tsah-vahn-yeh?)*

199. Are there any restaurants past security?
Да ли има ресторана после безбедносне контроле?
(Dah lee ee-mah rehs-toh-rah-nah pohs-leh behz-behd-nohs-neh kohn-troh-leh?)

200. What's the airport's Wi-Fi password?
Каква је шифра за Wi-Fi на аеродрому?
(Kahk-vah yeh shee-frah zah wee-fee nah ah-eh-roh-droh-moo?)

201. Can I bring duty-free items on board?
Могу ли унети бесцаринске ствари на брод?
(Moh-goo lee oo-neh-tee behs-tsah-reens-keh stvah-ree nah brohd?)

202. Is there a pharmacy at the airport?
Да ли постоји апотека на аеродрому?
(Dah lee poh-stoh-yee ah-poh-teh-kah nah ah-eh-roh-droh-moo?)

Traveling by Car

203. How do I pay tolls on the highway?
Како да платим путарину на аутопуту?
(Kah-koh dah plah-teem poo-tah-ree-noo nah ah-oo-toh-poo-too?)

204. Where can I find a car wash nearby?
Где могу пронаћи ауто праоницу у близини?
(Gdeh moh-goo proh-nah-chee ah-oo-toh prah-oh-nee-tsoo oo bleh-zee-nee?)

205. Are there electric vehicle charging stations?
Да ли има станица за пуњење електричних аутомобила?
(Dah lee ee-mah stah-nee-tsah zah pooh-nyeh-nyeh eh-lehk-treech-neeh ah-oo-toh-moh-bee-lah?)

206. Can I rent a GPS navigation system with the car?
Могу ли да изнајмим GPS навигацију са аутомобилом?
(Moh-goo lee dah eez-nah-y-meem Jee-Pee-Ess nah-vee-gah-tsee-yoo sah ah-oo-toh-moh-bee-lom?)

207. What's the cost of parking in the city center?
Колико кошта паркирање у центру града?
(Koh-lee-koh koh-shta pahr-kee-rah-nyeh oo tsehn-troo grah-dah?)

208. Do I need an international driving permit?
Да ли ми је потребна међународна возачка дозвола?
(Dah lee mee yeh poh-trehb-nah meh-joo-nah-rohd-nah voh-zahch-kah dohz-voh-lah?)

209. Is roadside assistance available?
Да ли постоји помоћ на путу?
(Dah lee poh-stoh-yee poh-moch nah poot-oo?)

210. Are there any traffic cameras on this route?
Да ли има саобраћајних камера на овој рути?
(Dah lee ee-mah sah-oh-brah-chah-ynee-kh kah-meh-rah nah oh-voy roo-tee?)

211. Can you recommend a reliable mechanic?
Можете ли препоручити поузданог механичара?
(Moh-zheh-teh lee preh-poh-roo-chee-tee poh-ooz-dah-nog meh-hah-neech-ah-rah?)

212. What's the speed limit in residential areas?
Какво је ограничење брзине у стамбеним подручјима?
(Kah-kvoh yeh oh-grah-nee-cheh-nyeh brzee-neh oo stahm-beh-neem poh-droo-ch-yee-mah?)

Airport Transfers and Shuttles

213. Where is the taxi stand located at the airport?
     Где се налази такси стајалиште на аеродрому?
     (Gdeh seh nah-lah-zee tahk-see stah-yah-leesh-teh nah ah-eh-roh-droh-moo?)

214. Do airport shuttles run 24/7?
     Да ли аеродромски шатли раде нон-стоп?
     (Dah lee ah-eh-roh-dom-skee shah-tlee rah-deh nohn-stop?)

     > **Idiomatic Expression:** "Пити као смук." -
     > Meaning: "To drink a lot."
     > (Literal translation: "To drink like a sponge.")

215. How long does it take to reach downtown by taxi?
     Колико времена је потребно да се таксијем стигне до центра града?
     (Koh-lee-koh vreh-myeh-nah yeh poh-trehb-noh dah seh tahk-see-yem stee-gneh doh tsehn-trah grah-dah?)

216. Is there a designated pick-up area for ride-sharing services?
     Да ли постоји одређено место за усуђивање услуга дељења вожње?
     (Dah lee poh-stoh-yee oh-dreh-jeh-noh meh-stoh zah oo-soo-jee-vah-nyeh oo-sloo-gah deh-lyeh-nyah vohzhy-eh?)

217. Can I book a shuttle in advance?
     Могу ли унапред резервисати шатл?
     (Moh-goo lee oo-nah-pred reh-zehr-vee-sah-tee shah-tl?)

     > **Fun Fact:** Ђаволја Варош, known as Devil's Town, features 202 unique rock formations.

218. Do hotels offer free shuttle service to the airport?
Да ли хотели нуде бесплатан трансфер до аеродрома?
(Dah lee hoh-teh-lee noo-deh beh-splah-tahn trahns-fehr doh ah-eh-roh-droh-mah?)

219. What's the rate for a private airport transfer?
Колико кошта приватни трансфер до аеродрома?
(Koh-lee-koh koh-shta pree-vat-nee trahns-fehr doh ah-eh-roh-droh-mah?)

220. Are there any public buses connecting to the airport?
Да ли постоје јавни аутобуси који иду до аеродрома?
(Dah lee poh-stoh-yeh yahv-nee ah-oo-toh-boo-see koh-yee ee-doo doh ah-eh-roh-droh-mah?)

221. Can you recommend a reliable limousine service?
Можете ли препоручити поуздану лимузинску услугу?
(Moh-zheh-teh lee preh-poh-roo-chee-tee poh-ooz-dah-noo lee-moo-zeen-skoo oo-sloo-goo?)

222. Is there an airport shuttle for early morning flights?
Да ли постоји шатл до аеродрома за ране летове?
(Dah lee poh-stoh-yee shah-tl doh ah-eh-roh-droh-mah zah rah-neh leh-toh-veh?)

Traveling with Luggage

223. Can I check my bags at this train station?
Могу ли да предам свој багаж на овој железничкој станици?
(Moh-goo lee dah preh-dahm svoy bah-gahzh nah oh-voy zheh-lez-neech-koy stah-nee-tsee?)

224.   Where can I find baggage carts in the airport?
Где могу пронаћи колица за багаж на аеродрому?
(Gdeh moh-goo proh-nah-chee koh-lee-tsah zah bah-gahzh nah ah-eh-roh-droh-moo?)

> **Fun Fact:** Serbia was home to some of the oldest Neolithic civilizations, including the Starčevo and Vinča cultures.

225.   Are there weight limits for checked baggage?
Да ли постоје ограничења тежине за предати багаж?
(Dah lee poh-stoh-yeh oh-grah-nee-cheh-nyah tez-ee-neh zah preh-dah-tee bah-gahzh?)

226.   Can I carry my backpack as a personal item?
Могу ли носити ранац као лични багаж?
(Moh-goo lee noh-see-tee rah-nats kah-oh leech-nee bah-gahzh?)

227.   What's the procedure for oversized luggage?
Какав је поступак за велики багаж?
(Kah-kahv yeh poh-stoo-pahk zah veh-lee-kee bah-gahzh?)

228.   Can I bring a stroller on the bus?
Могу ли унети колица за бебе у аутобус?
(Moh-goo lee oo-neh-tee koh-lee-tsah zah beh-beh oo ah-oo-toh-boos?)

229.   Are there lockers for storing luggage at the airport?
Да ли постоје ормарићи за складиштење багажа на аеродрому?
(Dah lee poh-stoh-yeh or-mah-ree-chee zah sklah-deesh-teh-nyeh bah-gahzh nah ah-eh-roh-droh-moo?)

> **Fun Fact:** The Serbian Crown Jewels are hidden and haven't been seen in over 70 years.

230. How do I label my luggage with contact information?
Како да означим свој багаж контактним информацијама?
(Kah-koh dah oh-znah-cheem svoy bah-gahzh kohn-tahkt-neem een-for-mah-tsee-yah-mah?)

231. Is there a lost and found office at the train station?
Да ли постоји канцеларија за изгубљене ствари на железничкој станици?
(Dah lee poh-stoh-yee kahn-tseh-lah-ree-yah zah eez-goo-blyeh-neh stvah-ree nah zheh-lez-neech-koy stah-nee-tsee?)

> **Idiomatic Expression:** "Висити о концу." -
> Meaning: "To hang by a thread (in a dangerous situation)."
> (Literal translation: "Hanging by a thread.")

232. Can I carry fragile items in my checked bags?
Могу ли унети крхке ствари у свој предати багаж?
(Moh-goo lee oo-neh-tee khrh-keh stvah-ree oo svoy preh-dah-tee bah-gahzh?)

> "Нема дима без ватре."
> **"There's no smoke without fire."**
> *If there's evidence of a problem,*
> *a problem likely exists.*

Word Search Puzzle: Travel & Transportation

AIRPORT
АЕРОДРОМ
BUS
АУТОБУС
TAXI
ТАКСИ
TICKET
КАРТА
MAP
МАПА
CAR
АУТО
METRO
МЕТРО
BICYCLE
БИЦИКЛ
DEPARTURE
ПОЛАЗАК
ARRIVAL
ДОЛАЗАК
ROAD
ПУТ
PLATFORM
ПЕРОН
STATION
СТАНИЦА
TERMINAL
ТЕРМИНАЛ

```
Y  K  U  R  U  D  R  O  H  N  F  О  Б  П  B
C  A  L  F  A  Y  R  A  X  W  X  T  И  E  T
E  P  Q  O  B  T  A  C  B  J  У  Ц  P  Z
O  T  R  P  E  O  S  N  W  P  C  A  И  O  Q
J  A  C  M  K  A  З  Л  O  П  Q  K  H  G
U  Z  У  C  P  E  Q  N  B  J  I  G  Л  H  C
U  G  Б  S  S  L  R  A  L  J  X  X  A  E  S
E  N  O  L  F  F  A  L  B  U  K  N  H  G  N
F  Z  T  U  L  Z  Q  T  G  V  E  N  И  J  Q
A  L  У  L  L  D  S  H  F  I  F  Q  M  Z  D
S  Q  A  L  C  T  H  E  J  O  S  A  P  Z  Q
J  R  S  U  A  Y  D  T  N  W  R  O  E  W  D
L  V  Y  T  U  N  M  E  T  P  O  M  T  O  K
G  A  I  J  C  B  I  P  B  Z  L  U  L  R  A
Y  O  V  P  S  M  A  M  T  I  E  M  Y  W  З
N  E  T  I  H  I  T  B  R  C  C  B  Q  W  A
R  G  K  F  R  R  O  I  A  E  A  Y  P  K  Л
F  L  G  P  B  R  C  Y  C  Z  T  S  C  D  O
V  L  O  G  S  I  A  U  K  K  P  X  E  Л  Д
V  R  M  O  P  Д  O  P  E  A  E  P  Q  T  E
T  G  J  A  П  A  M  T  P  W  A  T  K  Q  U
B  W  C  G  D  G  R  G  B  R  L  V  U  T  N
N  G  L  E  M  Y  S  I  T  U  R  M  C  H  Q
B  V  J  K  S  W  R  U  A  Ц  И  H  A  T  C
W  T  A  K  C  И  R  V  B  O  F  Q  M  F  L
R  R  S  W  W  E  Z  A  Q  P  I  A  I  C  N
П  У  T  B  C  D  Y  V  J  R  P  X  K  V  Q
V  H  Z  Q  I  X  H  I  W  Z  A  N  K  E  Q
V  Y  U  N  R  W  W  Z  V  T  N  Y  D  G  K
K  U  O  P  F  G  J  O  S  A  S  H  I  A  P
```

Correct Answers:

ACCOMMODATIONS

- CHECKING INTO A HOTEL -
- ASKING ABOUT ROOM AMENITIES -
- REPORTING ISSUES OR MAKING REQUESTS -

Hotel Check-In

233. I have a reservation under [Name].
Имам резервацију на име [Име].
(Ee-mahm reh-zehr-vah-tsee-yoo nah ee-meh [Ee-meh].)

234. Can I see some identification, please?
Могу ли да видим неки идентификациони документ, молим вас?
(Moh-goo lee dah vee-deem neh-kee ee-den-tee-fee-kah-tsee-oh-nee doh-koo-ment, moh-leem vahs?)

235. What time is check-in/check-out?
Када је пријава/одјава?
(Kah-dah yeh pree-yah-vah/ohd-yah-vah?)

236. Is breakfast included in the room rate?
Да ли је доручак укључен у цену собе?
(Dah lee yeh doh-roo-chak ooh-klyoo-chen oo tseh-noo soh-beh?)

237. Do you need a credit card for incidentals?
Да ли је потребна кредитна карта за додатне трошкове?
(Dah lee yeh poh-trehb-nah kreh-deet-nah kahr-tah zah doh-dah-tneh trohsh-koh-veh?)

238. May I have a room key, please?
Могу ли добити кључ од собе, молим вас?
(Moh-goo lee doh-bee-tee klyooch ohd soh-beh, moh-leem vahs?)

239. Is there a shuttle service to the airport?
Да ли постоји шатл услуга до аеродрома?
(Dah lee poh-stoh-yee shah-tl oo-sloo-gah doh ah-eh-roh-droh-mah?)

240.   Could you call a bellhop for assistance?
        Можете ли позвати носача за помоћ?
        (*Moh-zheh-teh lee pohz-vah-tee noh-sah-chah zah poh-moch?*)

> **Fun Fact:** Serbia is home to the oldest coffee shop in Europe, established in 1522.

Room Amenities

241.   Can I request a non-smoking room?
        Могу ли тражити собу за непушаче?
        (*Moh-goo lee trah-zhee-tee soh-boo zah neh-pooh-shah-cheh?*)

242.   Is there a mini-fridge in the room?
        Да ли у соби постоји мини-фрижидер?
        (*Dah lee oo soh-bee poh-stoh-yee mee-nee-free-zhee-dehr?*)

243.   Do you provide free Wi-Fi access?
        Да ли пружате бесплатан приступ Wi-Fi-jy?
        (*Dah lee proo-zhah-teh beh-splah-tahn prees-toop Vee-Fee-yoo?*)

244.   Can I have an extra pillow or blanket?
        Могу ли добити још један јастук или ћебе?
        (*Moh-goo lee doh-bee-tee yosh yeh-dahn yah-stook eely chyeh-beh?*)

245.   Is there a hairdryer in the bathroom?
        Да ли има фен у купатилу?
        (*Dah lee ee-mah fehn oo koo-pah-tee-loo?*)

246. What's the TV channel lineup?
Који су ТВ канали?
(*Koh-yee soo te-ve kah-nah-lee?*)

247. Are toiletries like shampoo provided?
Да ли се обезбеђују тоалетне потрепштине као шампон?
(*Dah lee seh oh-behz-beh-dzhoo-yoo toh-ah-leht-neh poh-trehp-shtee-neh kah-oh shahm-pohn?*)

248. Is room service available 24/7?
Да ли је услуга собне услуге доступна 24 сата дневно?
(*Dah lee yeh oo-sloo-gah sohb-neh oo-sloo-geh doh-stoo-pnah dva-deh-set cheh-ti-ree sah-tah dnehv-noh?*)

Fun Fact: Serbia had clock towers before Switzerland.

Reporting Issues

249. There's a problem with the air conditioning.
Има проблем са клима уређајем.
(*Ee-mah proh-blem sah klee-mah oo-reh-dzha-yem.*)

250. The shower is not working properly.
Туш не ради како треба.
(*Toosh neh rah-dee kah-koh treh-bah.*)

251. My room key card isn't functioning.
Моја картица за собу не функционише.
(*Moh-yah kahr-tee-tsah zah soh-boo neh foonk-tsee-oh-nee-sheh.*)

252. There's a leak in the bathroom.
Има цурење у купатилу.
(*Ee-mah tsoo-reh-nyeh oo koo-pah-tee-loo.*)

253. The TV remote is not responding.
Даљински за ТВ не реагује.
(*Dahl-yin-skee zah te-ve neh reh-ah-goo-ye.*)

254. Can you fix the broken light in my room?
Можете ли поправити покварену лампу у мојој соби?
(*Moh-zheh-teh lee poh-prah-vee-tee poh-kvah-reh-noo lahm-poo oo moh-yoy soh-bee?*)

255. I need assistance with my luggage.
Треба ми помоћ са мојим багажом.
(*Treh-bah mee poh-moch sah moh-yim bah-gah-zhom.*)

256. There's a strange noise coming from next door.
Долази чудан звук из суседне собе.
(*Doh-lah-zee choo-dahn zvook eez soo-sehd-neh soh-beh.*)

Making Requests

257. Can I have a wake-up call at 7 AM?
Могу ли добити будиљење у 7 ујутру?
(*Moh-goo lee doh-bee-tee boo-dee-lyeh-nyeh oo sedum oo-yoo-troo?*)

> **Fun Fact:** The word "vampire" is one of the few Serbian words that is used worldwide.

258. Please send extra towels to my room.
Молим вас, пошаљите додатне пешкире у моју собу.
(*Moh-leem vahs, poh-shah-lyee-teh doh-daht-neh peh-skee-reh oo moh-yoo soh-boo.*)

259. Could you arrange a taxi for tomorrow?
Можете ли организовати такси за сутра?
(*Moh-zheh-teh lee or-gah-nee-zoh-vah-tee tahk-see zah soo-trah?*)

260. I'd like to extend my stay for two more nights.
Желим да продужим боравак за још две ноћи.
(*Zheh-leem dah proh-doo-zheem boh-rah-vahk zah yosh dveh noh-chee.*)

> **Idiomatic Expression:** "Ићи као по лоју." -
> Meaning: "Everything is going smoothly."
> (Literal translation: "Going like on oil.")

261. Is it possible to change my room?
Да ли је могуће променити моју собу?
(*Dah lee yeh moh-goo-chyeh proh-meh-nee-tee moh-yoo soh-boo?*)

262. Can I have a late check-out at 2 PM?
Могу ли имати касни одлазак у 14 часова?
(*Moh-goo lee ee-mah-tee kahs-nee od-lah-zahk oo chet-ee-ree-nah-est chah-soh-vah?*)

263. I need an iron and ironing board.
Треба ми пегла и даска за пеглање.
(*Treh-bah mee peh-glah ee dah-skah zah peh-glah-nyeh.*)

264. Could you provide directions to [location]?
Можете ли ми дати упутства до [локације]?
(*Moh-zheh-teh lee mee dah-tee oo-poot-stvah doh [loh-kah-tsee-yeh]?*)

Room Types and Preferences

265. I'd like to book a single room, please.
Желим да резервишем једнокреветну собу, молим вас.
(*Zheh-leem dah reh-zer-vee-shehm yehd-noh-kreh-veh-tnoo soh-boo, moh-leem vahs.*)

266. Do you have any suites available?
Да ли имате слободних апартмана?
(*Dah lee ee-mah-teh sloh-bohd-neeh ah-pahrt-mah-nah?*)

267. Is there a room with a view of the city?
Да ли има соба са погледом на град?
(*Dah lee ee-mah soh-bah sah poh-gleh-dohm nah grahd?*)

268. Is breakfast included in the room rate?
Да ли је доручак укључен у цену собе?
(*Dah lee yeh doh-roo-chahk ooh-klyoo-chen oo tseh-noo soh-beh?*)

269. Can I request a room on a higher floor?
Могу ли затражити собу на вишем спрату?
(*Moh-goo lee zah-trah-zhee-tee soh-boo nah vee-shehm sprah-too?*)

270. Is there an option for a smoking room?
Да ли постоји опција за собу за пушаче?
(*Dah lee poh-stoh-yee op-tsee-yah zah soh-boo zah poo-shah-cheh?*)

> **Travel Story:** At the top of Belgrade's Avala Tower, a visitor exclaimed, "Све се види одавде!" translating to "You can see everything from herc!" marveling at the panoramic view.

271. Are there connecting rooms for families?
Да ли има повезаних соба за породице?
(*Dah lee ee-mah poh-veh-zah-neeh soh-bah zah poh-roh-dee-tseh?*)

272. I'd prefer a king-size bed.
Предпочитао/предпочитала бих кревет величине "кинг".
(*Prehd-poh-chee-tah-oh/prehd-poh-chee-tah-lah beeh kreh-veht veh-lee-chee-neh "keeng".*)

273. Is there a bathtub in any of the rooms?
Да ли у некој од соба постоји када?
(*Dah lee oo neh-koy od soh-bah poh-stoh-yee kah-dah?*)

Hotel Facilities and Services

274. What time does the hotel restaurant close?
До када ради ресторан хотела?
(*Doh kah-dah rah-dee rehs-toh-rahn hoh-teh-lah?*)

275. Is there a fitness center in the hotel?
Да ли у хотелу постоји фитнес центар?
(*Dah lee oo hoh-teh-loo poh-stoh-yee feet-nes tsehn-tahr?*)

276. Can I access the pool as a guest?
Да ли као гост могу да користим базен?
(*Dah lee kah-oh gohst moh-goo dah koh-ree-steem bah-zen?*)

277. Do you offer laundry facilities?
Да ли пружате услуге прања веша?
(*Dah lee proo-zha-teh oo-sloo-geh prah-nyah veh-shah?*)

278. Is parking available on-site?
Да ли је паркинг доступан у склопу хотела?
(*Dah lee yeh pahr-keeng doh-stoo-pahn oo skloh-poo hoh-teh-lah?*)

279. Is room cleaning provided daily?
Да ли се дневно чисте собе?
(*Dah lee seh dnehv-noh chees-teh soh-beh?*)

280. Can I use the business center?
Да ли могу да користим пословни центар?
(*Dah lee moh-goo dah koh-ree-steem poh-sloh-vnee tsehn-tahr?*)

281. Are pets allowed in the hotel?
Да ли су дозвољени кућни љубимци у хотелу?
(*Dah lee soo doh-zvoh-lyeh-nee kooch-nee lyoo-beem-tsee oo hoh-teh-loo?*)

> **Travel Story:** In a traditional Serbian household, a hostess offered homemade rakija with, "Домаћинска добродошлица," meaning "A homely welcome."

Payment and Check-Out

282. Can I have the bill, please?
Могу ли добити рачун, молим вас?
(*Moh-goo lee doh-bee-tee rah-choon, moh-leem vahs?*)

283. Do you accept credit cards?
Да ли прихватате кредитне картице?
(*Dah lee pree-hvah-tah-teh kreh-deet-neh kahr-tee-tseh?*)

284. Can I pay in cash?
Могу ли платити готовином?
(*Moh-goo lee plah-tee-tee goh-toh-vee-nohm?*)

285. Is there a security deposit required?
Да ли је потребан депозит за сигурност?
(*Dah lee yeh poh-treh-bahn deh-poh-zeet zah see-goor-nost?*)

286. Can I get a receipt for my stay?
Могу ли добити потврду за мој боравак?
(*Moh-goo lee doh-bee-tee poh-tvruh-doo zah moy boh-rah-vahk?*)

287. What's the check-out time?
Када је време за одјаву?
(*Kah-dah yeh vreh-meh zah ohd-yah-voo?*)

288. Is late check-out an option?
Да ли је могућ касан одлазак?
(*Dah lee yeh moh-gooch kah-sahn ohd-lah-zahk?*)

289. Can I settle my bill in advance?
Могу ли унапред платити свој рачун?
(*Moh-goo lee oo-nah-pred plah-tee-tee svoy rah-choon?*)

Booking Accommodations

290. Can I book online or by phone?
Могу ли резервисати онлајн или путем телефона?
(*Moh-goo lee reh-zer-vee-sah-tee ohn-lahyn eely poh-tem teh-leh-foh-nah?*)

291. How much is the room rate per night?
Колико кошта соба по ноћи?
(*Koh-lee-koh koh-shtah soh-bah poh noh-chee?*)

292. I'd like to make a reservation.
Желим да направим резервацију.
(*Zheh-leem dah nah-prah-veem reh-zer-vah-tsee-yoo.*)

293. Are there any special promotions?
Да ли постоје неке специјалне промоције?
(*Dah lee poh-stoh-yeh neh-keh speh-tsee-yahl-neh proh-moh-tsee-yeh?*)

294. Is breakfast included in the booking?
Да ли је доручак укључен у резервацији?
(*Dah lee yeh doh-roo-chahk ooh-klyoo-chen oo reh-zer-vah-tsee-yee?*)

295. Can you confirm my reservation?
Можете ли потврдити моју резервацију?
(*Moh-zheh-teh lee poh-tvur-dee-tee moh-yoo reh-zer-vah-tsee-yoo?*)

296. What's the cancellation policy?
Каква је политика отказивања?
(*Kah-kvah yeh poh-lee-tee-kah oht-kah-zee-vah-nyah?*)

297. I'd like to modify my booking.
Желим да изменим своју резервацију.
(*Zheh-leem dah eez-meh-neem svoh-yoo reh-zer-vah-tsee-yoo.*)

> "Није злато све што сија."
> **"Not all that glitters is gold."**
> *Things that appear valuable or true might not be so.*

Mini Lesson:
Basic Grammar Principles in Serbian #1

Introduction:

Serbian, written in both Cyrillic and Latin alphabets, is a South Slavic language primarily spoken in Serbia and regions of the Balkans. Its grammar is rich and complex, offering both challenges and rewards to learners. This lesson introduces key concepts of Serbian grammar, essential for beginners.

1. Nouns and Gender:

Serbian nouns are divided into three genders: masculine, feminine, and neuter. The gender of a noun influences its behavior in different cases.

- *Masculine: пас (dog)*
- *Feminine: кућа (house)*
- *Neuter: језеро (lake)*

2. The Case System:

Serbian has seven cases which affect nouns, pronouns, and adjectives: nominative, genitive, dative, accusative, vocative, instrumental, and locative.

- *Nominative: пас (as a subject)*
- *Accusative: пса (as a direct object)*

3. Personal Pronouns:

Personal pronouns in Serbian vary according to case:

- *Ja (I)*
- *Tu (you - singular)*
- *Он/Она/Оно (he/she/it)*
- *Mu (we)*
- *Bu (you - plural)*
- *Они/Оне/Она (they - masculine/feminine/neuter)*

4. Verb Conjugation:

Verbs are conjugated based on tense, mood, person, and number, with no infinitive form.

- *читам (I read)*
- *читаш (You read)*

5. Tenses:

Focus initially on present, past, and future tenses:

- *Present: читам (I read)*
- *Past: читао/читала/читало сам (I read - masculine/feminine/neuter)*
- *Future: hy читати (I will read)*

6. Negation:

Negation is generally formed by placing 'не' before the verb:

- *Не читам (I don't read)*

7. Questions:

Form questions using intonation or question words like 'ко' (who), 'шта' (what), 'где' (where), 'када' (when), 'како' (how):

- *Читаш ли ти књигу? (Are you reading the book?)*

8. Plurals:

Plurals in Serbian can vary based on gender and the ending of the noun:

- *пас > пси (dogs)*
- *кућа > куће (houses)*

Conclusion:

This overview of Serbian grammar is just the beginning. As you dive deeper, you'll encounter more complex structures. Consistent practice and exposure to the language are key to mastering Serbian. Срећно! (Good luck!)

SHOPPING

- BARGAINING AND HAGGLING -
- DESCRIBING ITEMS AND SIZES -
- MAKING PURCHASES AND PAYMENTS -

Bargaining

298. Can you give me a discount?
Можете ли ми дати попуст?
(Moh-zheh-teh lee mee dah-tee poh-poost?)

299. What's your best price?
Која је ваша најбоља цена?
(Koh-yah yeh vah-shah nigh-boh-lyah tseh-nah?)

300. Is this the final price?
Да ли је ово коначна цена?
(Dah lee yeh oh-voh koh-nach-nah tseh-nah?)

301. What's the lowest you can go?
Која је најнижа цена коју можете понудити?
(Koh-yah yeh nigh-nee-zhah tseh-nah koh-yoo moh-zheh-teh poh-noo-dee-tee?)

302. Do you offer any discounts for cash payments?
Да ли нудите попусте за готовинско плаћање?
(Dah lee noo-dee-teh poh-poos-teh zah goh-toh-veen-skoh plah-chah-nyeh?)

303. Are there any promotions or deals?
Да ли има неких промоција или попуста?
(Dah lee ee-mah neh-kee-kh proh-moh-tsee-yah eely poh-poos-tah?)

304. I'm on a budget. Can you lower the price?
Имам ограничен буџет. Можете ли снизити цену?
(Ee-mahm oh-grah-nee-chen booj-et. Moh-zheh-teh lee snee-zee-tee tseh-noo?)

305. I'd like to negotiate the price.
Желим да преговарам о цени.
(*Zheh-leem dah preh-goh-vah-rahm oh tseh-nee.*)

306. Can you do any better on the price?
Можете ли понудити бољу цену?
(*Moh-zheh-teh lee poh-noo-dee-tee boh-lyoo tseh-noo?*)

307. Can you match the price from your competitor?
Можете ли ускладити цену са ценом вашег конкурента?
(*Moh-zheh-teh lee oos-klah-dee-tee tseh-noo sah tseh-nohm vah-shehg kohn-koo-ren-tah?*)

Item Descriptions

308. Can you tell me about this product?
Можете ли ми рећи нешто више о овом производу?
(*Moh-zheh-teh lee mee reh-chee neh-shtoh vee-sheh oh oh-vohm proh-ees-voh-doo?*)

309. What are the specifications of this item?
Какве су спецификације овог производа?
(*Kah-kveh soo speh-tsee-fee-kah-tsee-yeh oh-vohg proh-ees-voh-dah?*)

310. Is this available in different colors?
Да ли је ово доступно у различитим бојама?
(*Dah lee yeh oh-voh doh-stoo-pnoh oo rahz-lee-chee-teem boh-yah-mah?*)

311. Can you explain how this works?
Можете ли објаснити како ово функционише?
(*Moh-zheh-teh lee ob-yah-snee-tee kah-koh oh-voh foonk-tsee-oh-nee-sheh?*)

312.   What's the material of this item?
Од каквог је материјала направљен овај производ?
(*Od kah-kvohg yeh mah-teh-ree-yah-lah nah-prahv-lyen oh-vigh proh-eez-vohd?*)

313.   Are there any warranties or guarantees?
Да ли постоје гаранције или гаранција за овај производ?
(*Dah lee poh-stoh-yeh gah-ran-tsee-yeh eely gah-ran-tsee-yah zah oh-vigh proh-eez-vohd?*)

314.   Does it come with accessories?
Да ли се испоручује са додацима?
(*Dah lee seh ees-poh-roo-choo-yeh sah doh-dah-tsee-mah?*)

315.   Can you show me how to use this?
Можете ли ми показати како се користи ово?
(*Moh-zheh-teh lee mee poh-kah-zah-tee kah-koh seh koh-ree-stee oh-voh?*)

316.   Are there any size options available?
Да ли постоје различите величине?
(*Dah lee poh-stoh-yeh rahz-lee-chee-teh veh-lee-chee-neh?*)

317.   Can you describe the features of this product?
Можете ли описати карактеристике овог производа?
(*Moh-zheh-teh lee oh-pee-sah-tee kah-rahk-teh-ree-stee-keh oh-vohg proh-eez-voh-dah?*)

Payments

318.   I'd like to pay with a credit card.
Желим да платим кредитном картицом.
(*Zheh-leem dah plah-teem kreh-deet-nom kahr-tee-tsohm.*)

319. Do you accept debit cards?
Да ли прихватате дебитне картице?
(*Dah lee pree-hvah-tah-teh deh-beet-neh kahr-tee-tseh?*)

320. Can I pay in cash?
Могу ли платити готовином?
(*Moh-goo lee plah-tee-tee goh-toh-vee-nohm?*)

> **Idiomatic Expression:** "Нема зиме." -
> Meaning: "No worries."
> (Literal translation: "There's no winter.")

321. What's your preferred payment method?
Који је ваш преферирани начин плаћања?
(*Koh-yee yeh vahsh preh-feh-ree-rah-nee nah-cheen plah-chah-nyah?*)

322. Is there an extra charge for using a card?
Да ли има додатних трошкова за коришћење картице?
(*Dah lee ee-mah doh-dah-tnih trohsh-koh-vah zah koh-reesh-cheh-nyeh kahr-tee-tseh?*)

323. Can I split the payment into installments?
Могу ли разложити плаћање на рате?
(*Moh-goo lee rahz-loh-zhee-tee plah-chah-nyeh nah rah-teh?*)

324. Do you offer online payment options?
Да ли нудите могућности онлајн плаћања?
(*Dah lee noo-dee-teh moh gooch nos-tce ohn-lighn plah-chah-nyah?*)

325. Can I get a receipt for this purchase?
Могу ли добити фискални рачун за ову куповину?
(*Moh-goo lee doh-bee-tee fees-kahl-nee rah-choon zah oh-voo koo-poh-vee-noo?*)

326.   Are there any additional fees?
       Да ли има додатних такси?
       (*Dah lee ee-mah doh-dah-tnih tahk-see?*)

327.   Is there a minimum purchase amount for card payments?
       Да ли постоји минимални износ за плаћање картицом?
       (*Dah lee poh-stoh-yee mee-nee-mahl-nee eez-nos zah
       plah-chah-nyeh kahr-tee-tsohm?*)

> **Travel Story:** On the streets of historic Stari Grad in
> Belgrade, a passerby said, "Овај град дише историју,"
> meaning "This city breathes history."

Asking for Recommendations

328.   Can you recommend something popular?
       Можете ли препоручити нешто популарно?
       (*Moh-zheh-teh lee preh-poh-roo-chee-tee neh-shtoh
       poh-poo-lahr-noh?*)

329.   What's your best-selling product?
       Који је ваш најпродаванији производ?
       (*Koy-yee yeh vahsh nigh-proh-dah-vah-nee-yee proh-eez-vohd?*)

330.   Do you have any customer favorites?
       Да ли имате неке омиљене производе код купаца?
       (*Dah lee ee-mah-teh neh-keh oh-mee-lyeh-neh proh-eez-voh-deh
       kohd koo-pah-tsah?*)

331.   Is there a brand you would suggest?
       Да ли бисте препоручили неки бренд?
       (*Dah lee bees-teh preh-poh-roo-chee-lee neh-kee brehnd?*)

332. Could you point me to high-quality items?
      Можете ли ми указати на производе високог квалитета?
      (*Moh-zheh-teh lee mee oo-kah-zah-tee nah proh-eez-voh-deh
      vee-soh-kohg kvah-lee-teh-tah?*)

333. What do most people choose in this category?
      Шта већина људи бира у овој категорији?
      (*Shta veh-chee-nah lyoo-dee bee-rah oo oh-voy kah-teh-goh-ree-
      yee?*)

334. Are there any special recommendations?
      Да ли има неких посебних препорука?
      (*Dah lee ee-mah neh-kee-kh poh-sehb-neeh preh-poh-roo-kah?*)

335. Can you tell me what's trendy right now?
      Можете ли ми рећи шта је тренутно у моди?
      (*Moh-zheh-teh lee mee reh-chee shta yeh treh-noo-tnoh oo
      moh-dee?*)

336. What's your personal favorite here?
      Који је ваш лични фаворит овде?
      (*Koy-yee yeh vahsh lee-chnee fah-voh-reet ohv-deh?*)

337. Any suggestions for a gift?
      Имате ли неке предлоге за поклон?
      (*Ee-mah-teh lee neh-keh prehd-loh-geh zah poh-klohn?*)

          Language Learning Tip: Plan a Trip to Serbia -
          Immersion is one of the best ways to learn a language.

Returns and Exchanges

338. I'd like to return this item.
Желим да вратим овај производ.
(*Zheh-leem dah vrah-teem oh-vigh proh-eez-vohd.*)

339. Can I exchange this for a different size?
Могу ли да заменим ово за другу величину?
(*Moh-goo lee dah zah-meh-neem oh-voh zah droo-goo veh-lee-chee-noo?*)

340. What's your return policy?
Каква је ваша политика повраћаја?
(*Kah-kvah yeh vah-shah poh-lee-tee-kah pohv-rah-chigh-ah?*)

341. Is there a time limit for returns?
Да ли постоји временски ограничење за повраћај?
(*Dah lee poh-stoh-yee vreh-mehn-skee oh-grah-nee-cheh-nyeh zah pohv-rah-chigh?*)

342. Do I need a receipt for a return?
Да ли ми треба фискални рачун за повраћај?
(*Dah lee mee treh-bah fees-kahl-nee rah-choon zah pohv-rah-chigh?*)

343. Is there a restocking fee for returns?
Да ли има таксу за поновно снабдевање при повраћају?
(*Dah lee ee-mah tahk-soo zah poh-nov-noh snahb-deh-vah-nyeh pree pohv-rah-chigh-oo?*)

344. Can I get a refund or store credit?
Могу ли добити повраћај новца или кредит у радњи?
(*Moh-goo lee doh-bee-tee pohv-rah-chigh nov-tsah eely kreh-diht oo rahd-nyee?*)

345. Do you offer exchanges without receipts?
Да ли нудите замену без рачуна?
(*Dah lee noo-dee-teh zah-meh-noo behz rah-choo-nah?*)

346. What's the process for returning a defective item?
Какав је поступак за враћање неисправног производа?
(*Kah-kahv yeh poh-stoo-pahk zah vrah-chah-nyeh neh-ees-prahv-nohg proh-eez-voh-dah?*)

347. Can I return an online purchase in-store?
Могу ли вратити онлајн куповину у продавници?
(*Moh-goo lee vrah-tee-tee ohn-lighn koo-poh-vee-noo oo proh-dahv-nee-tsee?*)

> **Travel Story:** At a monastery in Fruška Gora, a monk described the serene environment as, "Мир који се ретко налази," translating to "A peace that is rarely found."

Shopping for Souvenirs

348. I'm looking for local souvenirs.
Тражим локалне сувенире.
(*Trah-zheem loh-kahl-neh soo-veh-neer-eh.*)

349. What's a popular souvenir from this place?
Који је популаран сувенир са овог места?
(*Koy-yee yeh poh-poo-lah-rahn soo-veh-neer sah oh-vog meh-stah?*)

350. Do you have any handmade souvenirs?
Да ли имате ручно рађене сувенире?
(*Dah lee ee-mah-teh rooch-noh rah-dye-neh soo-veh-neer-eh?*)

351. Are there any traditional items here?
Има ли овде традиционалних предмета?
(*Ee-mah lee ohv-deh trah-dee-tsee-oh-nahl-neeh prehd-meh-tah?*)

352. Can you suggest a unique souvenir?
Можете ли да предложите јединствени сувенир?
(*Moh-zheh-teh lee dah prehd-loh-zhee-teh yeh-deen-stveh-nee soo-veh-neer?*)

353. I want something that represents this city.
Желим нешто што представља овај град.
(*Zheh-leem neh-shtoh shtoh prehd-stahv-lyah oh-vigh grahd.*)

354. Are there souvenirs for a specific landmark?
Има ли сувенира за одређену знаменитост?
(*Ee-mah lee soo-veh-nee-rah zah oh-dreh-dye-noo zna-meh-nee-tost?*)

355. Can you show me souvenirs with cultural significance?
Можете ли ми показати сувенире са културним значајем?
(*Moh-zheh-teh lee mee poh-kah-zah-tee soo-veh-nee-reh sah kool-toor-neem zna-chigh-yem?*)

356. Do you offer personalized souvenirs?
Да ли нудите персонализоване сувенире?
(*Dah lee noo-dee-teh pehr-soh-nah-lee-zoh-vah-neh soo-veh-nee-reh?*)

357. What's the price range for souvenirs?
Какав је ценовни распон за сувенире?
(*Kah-kahv yeh tseh-nohv-nee rahs-pohn zah soo-veh-nee-reh?*)

Shopping Online

358. How do I place an order online?
Како да наручим онлајн?
(*Kah-koh dah nah-roo-cheem ohn-lighn?*)

359. What's the website for online shopping?
Какав је вебсајт за онлајн куповину?
(*Kah-kahv yeh vehb-sigh-t zah ohn-lighn koo-poh-vee-noo?*)

360. Do you offer free shipping?
Да ли нудите бесплатну доставу?
(*Dah lee noo-dee-teh behs-plaht-noo doh-stah-voo?*)

361. Are there any online discounts or promotions?
Да ли има онлајн попуста или промоција?
(*Dah lee ee-mah ohn-lighn poh-poos-tah eely proh-moh-tsee-yah?*)

362. Can I track my online order?
Могу ли пратити своју онлајн наруџбину?
(*Moh-goo lee prah-tee-tee svoh-yoo ohn-lighn nah-roo-dzbee-noo?*)

363. What's the return policy for online purchases?
Каква је политика повраћаја за онлајн куповине?
(*Kahk-vah yeh poh-lee-tee-kah pohv-rah-chigh-yah zah ohn-lighn koo-poh-vee-neh?*)

364. Do you accept various payment methods online?
Да ли прихватате различите методе плаћања онлајн?
(*Dah lee preeh-vah-tah-teh rahz-lee-chee-tch mch-toh-deh plah-chah-nyah ohn-lighn?*)

365. Is there a customer support hotline for online orders?
Да ли постоји линија подршке за клијенте за онлајн наручивање?
(*Ee-mah lee goh-resht-ah lee-nee-yah zah pod-druhzh-kah nah klee-en-tee zah on-line poh-ruhch-kee?*)

> **Idiomatic Expression:** "Бацити дрва у воду." - Meaning: "To give up."
> (Literal translation: "To throw wood into the water.")

366. Can I change or cancel my online order?
Могу ли да променим или откажем моју онлајн наруџбину?
(*Moh-goo lee dah proh-meh-neem eely oht-kah-zhem moh-yoo ohn-lighn nah-roo-dzh-bee-noo?*)

367. What's the delivery time for online purchases?
Колико времена траје достава за онлајн куповине?
(*Koh-lee-koh vreh-meh-nah trah-yeh doh-stah-vah zah ohn-lighn koo-poh-vee-neh?*)

> "Није сваки дан празник."
> **"Not every day is a holiday."**
> *Life isn't always easy or pleasant.*

Cross Word Puzzle: Shopping

(Provide the English translation for the following Serbian words)

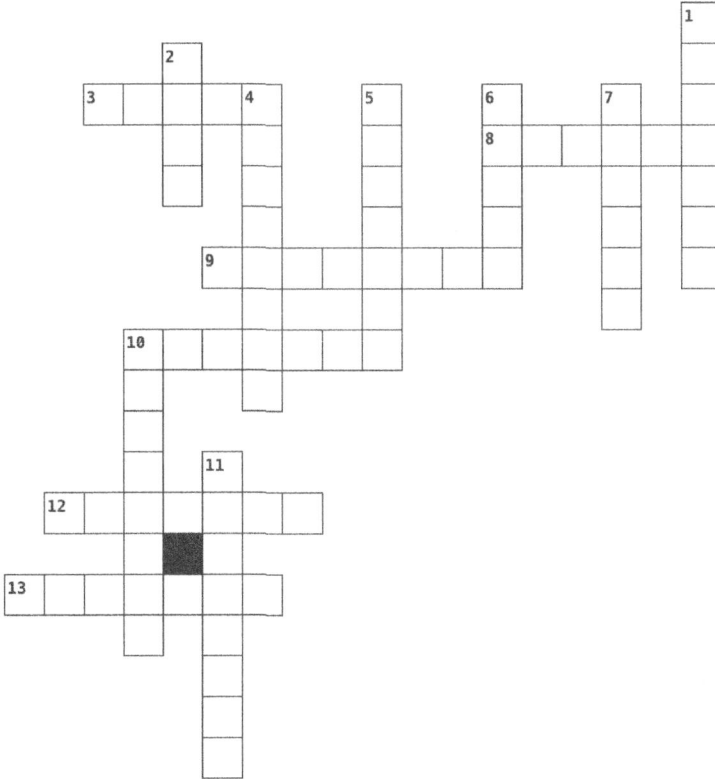

Down

1. - КОЛИЦА
2. - РАСПРОДАЈА
4. - ПОПУСТ
5. - БЛАГАЈНИК
6. - ЦЕНА
7. - НОВЧАНИК
10. - КУПАЦ
11. - КУПОВИНА

Across

3. - МАРКА
8. - МАЛОПРОДАЈА
9. - БУТИК
10. - ШАЛТЕР
12. - ОДЕЋА
13. - ФИСКАЛНИ РАЧУН

Correct Answers:

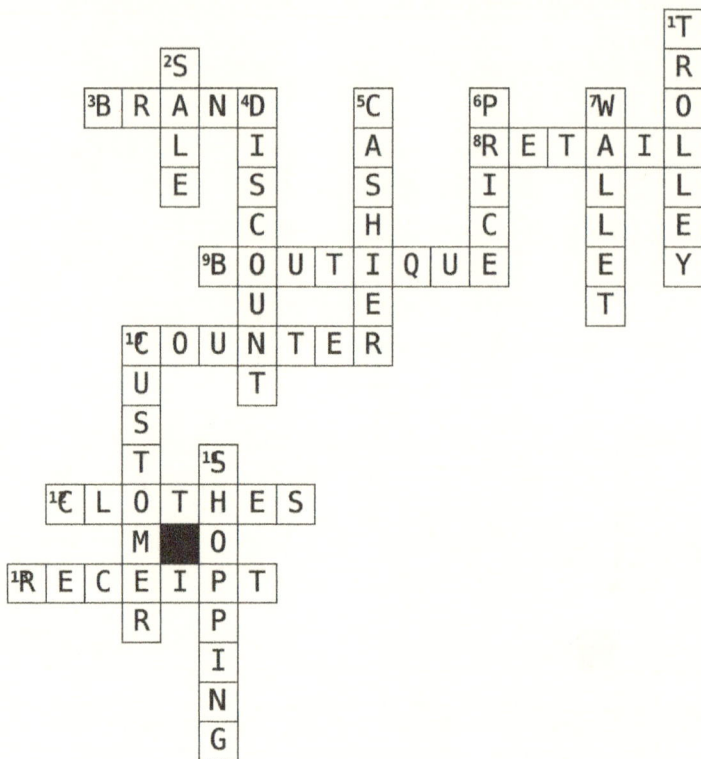

EMERGENCIES

- SEEKING HELP IN CASE OF AN EMERGENCY -
- REPORTING ACCIDENTS OR HEALTH ISSUES -
- CONTACTING AUTHORITIES OR MEDICAL SERVICES -

Getting Help in Emergencies

368. Call an ambulance, please.
Молим вас, позовите хитну помоћ.
(*Moh-leem vahs, poh-zoh-vee-teh heet-noo poh-moch.*)

> **Language Learning Tip:** Use Serbian Language Podcasts
> - Listen to podcasts for different proficiency levels.

369. I need a doctor right away.
Треба ми доктор одмах.
(*Treh-bah mee dohk-tor od-mah.*)

370. Is there a hospital nearby?
Да ли је болница у близини?
(*Dah lee yeh bohl-nee-tsah oo blee-zee-nee?*)

371. Help! I've lost my way.
У помоћ! Загубио сам пут.
(*Oo poh-moch! Zah-goo-bee-oh sahm poot.*)

372. Can you call the police?
Можете ли позвати полицију?
(*Moh-zheh-teh lee pohz-vah-tee poh-lee-tsee-yoo?*)

373. Someone, please call for help.
Неко, молим вас, позовите за помоћ.
(*Neh-koh, moh-leem vahs, poh-zoh-vee-teh zah poh-moch.*)

374. My friend is hurt, we need assistance.
Мој пријатељ је повређен, треба нам помоћ.
(*Moy pree-yah-tehl yeh poh-vreh-dye-en, treh-bah nahm poh-moch.*)

375. I've been robbed; I need the authorities.
Опљачкан сам; потребни су ми органи.
(*Oplyah-ckahn sahm; poh-trehb-nee soo mee or-gah-nee.*)

376. Please, I need immediate assistance.
Молим вас, потребна ми је хитна помоћ.
(*Moh-leem vahs, poh-trehb-nah mee yeh heet-nah poh-moch.*)

377. Is there a fire station nearby?
Да ли има ватрогасна станица у близини?
(*Dah lee ee-mah vah-troh-gahs-nah stah-nee-tsah oo blee-zee-nee?*)

Reporting Incidents

378. I've witnessed an accident.
Сведок сам био несреће.
(*Sveh-dohk sahm bee-oh neh-sreh-cheh.*)

379. There's been a car crash.
Дошло је до саобраћајне несреће.
(*Doh-shloh yeh doh sah-oh-brah-chigh-ne neh-sreh-cheh.*)

380. We need to report a fire.
Морамо да пријавимо пожар.
(*Moh-rah-moh dah pree-yah-vee-moh poh-zhar.*)

381. Someone has stolen my wallet.
Неко ми је украо новчаник.
(*Neh-koh mee yeh oo-krah-oh nov-cha-neek.*)

382. I need to report a lost passport.
Треба да пријавим изгубљени пасош.
(*Treh-bah dah pree-yah-veem eez-goo-blyeh-nee pah-sohsh.*)

383. There's a suspicious person here.
Овде има сумњива особа.
(*Ov-deh ee-mah soom-nyee-vah oh-soh-bah.*)

384. I've found a lost child.
Пронашао сам изгубљено дете.
(*Proh-nah-shaoh sahm eez-goo-blyeh-noh deh-teh.*)

385. Can you help me report a missing person?
Можете ли ми помоћи да пријавим несталу особу?
(*Moh-zheh-teh lee mee poh-mo-chi dah pree-yah-veem neh-stah-loo oh-soh-boo?*)

386. We've had a break-in at our home.
Дошло је до провале у нашој кући.
(*Doh-shloh yeh doh proh-vah-leh oo nah-shoy koo-chi.*)

387. I need to report a damaged vehicle.
Треба да пријавим оштећено возило.
(*Treh-bah dah pree-yah-veem oh-shteh-cheh-noh voh-zee-loh.*)

Contacting Authorities

388. I'd like to speak to the police.
Желим да разговарам са полицијом.
(*Zheh-leem dah rahz-goh-vah-rahm sah poh-lee-tsee-yohm.*)

389. I need to contact the embassy.
Треба да контактирам амбасаду.
(*Treh-bah dah kohn-tahk-teer-ahm ahm-bah-sah-doo.*)

390. Can you connect me to the fire department?
Можете ли ме повезати са ватрогасном службом?
(*Moh-zheh-teh lee meh poh-veh-zah-tee sah vah-troh-gahs-nohm sloozh-bohm?*)

391. We need to reach animal control.
Треба да контактирамо службу за контролу животиња.
(*Treh-bah dah kohn-tahk-teer-ah-moh sloozh-boo zah kohn-troh-loo zhee-voh-teen-yah.*)

392. How do I get in touch with the coast guard?
Како да контактирам обалску стражу?
(*Kah-koh dah kohn-tahk-teer-ahm oh-bahl-skoo strah-zhoo?*)

393. I'd like to report a noise complaint.
Желим да пријавим жалбу због буке.
(*Zheh-leem dah pree-yah-veem zhahl-boo zbohg boo-keh.*)

394. I need to contact child protective services.
Треба да контактирам службу за заштиту деце.
(*Treh-bah dah kohn-tahk-teer-ahm sloozh-boo zah zah-shtee-too deh-tseh.*)

395. Is there a hotline for disaster relief?
Да ли постоји линија за помоћ у катастрофама?
(*Dah lee poh-stoh-yee lee-nee-yah zah poh-moch oo kah-tah-stroh-fah-mah?*)

Fun Fact: Serbian is one of the easiest languages to read due to its phonetic nature.

396. I want to report a hazardous situation.
      Желим да пријавим опасну ситуацију.
      (*Zheh-leem dah pree-yah-veem oh-pahs-noo see-too-ah-tsee-yoo.*)

397. I need to reach the environmental agency.
      Потребно ми је да контактирам агенцију за животну средину.
      (*Poh-trehb-noh mee yeh dah kohn-tahk-teer-ahm ah-gen-tsee-yoo zah zhee-vot-noo sreh-dee-noo.*)

> **Travel Story:** During a traditional Serbian Slava (family feast day), a guest expressed the joy of the occasion with, "Ово је права фамилијарна атмосфера," meaning "This is a true family atmosphere."

Medical Emergencies

398. I'm feeling very ill.
      Осећам се врло лоше.
      (*Oh-seh-chahm seh vrloh loh-sheh.*)

399. There's been an accident; we need a medic.
      Дошло је до несреће; потребан нам је лекар.
      (*Doh-shloh yeh doh neh-sreh-cheh; poh-treh-bahn nahm yeh leh-kahr.*)

400. Call 112; it's a medical emergency.
      Позовите 112; у питању је медицинска хитност.
      (*Poh-zoh-vee-teh sto edin dva; oo pee-tah-nyoo yeh meh-dee-tseen-skah heet-nost.*)

> **Fun Fact:** Serbian is the only European language that actively uses two different scripts: Cyrillic and Latin.

401.   We need an ambulance right away.
      Треба нам хитна помоћ одмах.
      (*Treh-bah nahm heet-nah poh-moch od-mah.*)

402.   I'm having trouble breathing.
      Имам проблема са дисањем.
      (*Ee-mahm proh-bleh-mah sah dee-sah-nyehm.*)

403.   Someone has lost consciousness.
      Неко је изгубио свест.
      (*Neh-koh yeh eez-goo-bee-oh svehst.*)

404.   I think it's a heart attack; call for help.
      Мислим да је срчани удар; позовите у помоћ.
      (*Mees-leem dah yeh sr-chah-nee oo-dahr; poh-zoh-vee-teh oo poh-moch.*)

405.   There's been a severe injury.
      Дошло је до озбиљне повреде.
      (*Doh-shloh yeh doh ohz-beel-nyeh poh-vreh-deh.*)

406.   I need immediate medical attention.
      Потребна ми је хитна медицинска помоћ.
      (*Poh-trehb-nah mee yeh heet-nah meh-dee-tseen-skah poh-moch.*)

407.   Is there a first-aid station nearby?
      Да ли је у близини станица прве помоћи?
      (*Dah lee yeh oo bleh-zee-nee stah-nee-tsah pur-veh poh-moch-ee?*)

> **Idiomatic Expression:** "Као куче у џаку." -
> Meaning: "To feel trapped or helpless."
> (Literal translation: "Like a dog in a sack.")

Fire and Safety

408. There's a fire; call 112!
Има пожар; позовите 112!
(*Ee-mah poh-zhar; poh-zoh-vee-teh sto edin dva!*)

409. We need to evacuate the building.
Морамо евакуисати зграду.
(*Moh-rah-moh eh-vah-koo-ee-sah-tee zgrah-doo.*)

410. Fire extinguisher, quick!
Ватрогасац, брзо!
(*Vah-troh-gah-sahts, brzoh!*)

411. I smell gas; we need to leave.
Осећам гас; морамо ићи.
(*Oh-seh-chahm gahs; moh-rah-moh ee-chee.*)

> **Fun Fact:** Serbian contains words from Old Church Slavonic, the first Slavic literary language.

412. Can you contact the fire department?
Можете ли контактирати ватрогасну службу?
(*Moh-zheh-teh lee kohn-tahk-tee-rah-tee vah-troh-gahs-noo sloozh-boo?*)

413. There's a hazardous spill; we need help.
Дошло је до опасног проливања; треба нам помоћ.
(*Doh-shloh yeh doh oh-pahs-nohg proh-lee-vah-nyah; treh-bah nahm poh-moch.*)

414. Is there a fire escape route?
Постоји ли пут за бекство од пожара?
(*Poh-stoh-yee lee poot zah behk-stvoh od poh-zhah-rah?*)

415. This area is not safe; we need to move.
Ово подручје није безбедно; треба да се померимо.
(*O-voh poh-drooch-ye nee-yeh behz-behd-noh; treh-bah dah seh poh-meh-ree-moh.*)

416. Alert, there's a potential explosion.
Упозорење, постоји могућност експлозије.
(*Oo-poh-zoh-reh-nyeh, poh-stoh-yee moh-gooch-nost ehks-ploh-zee-yeh.*)

417. I see smoke; we need assistance.
Видим дим; потребна нам је помоћ.
(*Vee-deem deem; poh-trehb-nah nahm yeh poh-moch.*)

Natural Disasters

418. It's an earthquake; take cover!
Земљотрес је; склоните се!
(*Zehm-lyoh-tres yeh; skloh-nee-teh seh!*)

419. We're experiencing a tornado; find shelter.
Дошло је до торнада; потражите склониште.
(*Doh-shloh yeh doh tor-nah-dah; poh-trah-zhee-teh skloh-neesh-teh.*)

420. Flood warning; move to higher ground.
Упозорење на поплаву; идите на више терене.
(*Oo-poh-zoh-reh-nyeh nah poh-plah-voo; ee-dee-teh nah vee-sheh teh-reh-neh.*)

421. We need to prepare for a hurricane.
Треба да се припремимо за ураган.
(*Treh-bah dah seh pree-preh-mee-moh zah oo-rah-gahn.*)

422. This is a tsunami alert; head inland.
Ово је упозорење на цунами; идите унутра у земљу.
(*O-voh yeh oo-poh-zoh-reh-nyeh nah tsoo-nah-mee; ee-dee-teh oo-noo-trah oo zem-lyoo.*)

> **Fun Fact:** Serbian has two dialectal forms based on the pronunciation of the word for 'what'.

423. It's a wildfire; evacuate immediately.
Ово је шумски пожар; хитно евакуишите се.
(*O-voh yeh shoom-skee poh-zhar; heet-noh eh-vah-koo-ee-shee-teh seh.*)

424. There's a volcanic eruption; take precautions.
Има вулканска ерупција; предузмите предострожности.
(*Ee-mah vool-kahn-skah eh-roop-tsee-yah; preh-doo-zmee-teh preh-doh-strozh-nohs-tee.*)

425. We've had an avalanche; help needed.
Дошло је до лавине; потребна је помоћ.
(*Doh-shloh yeh doh lah-vee-neh; poh-trehb-nah yeh poh-moch.*)

426. Earthquake aftershock; stay indoors.
Последице земљотреса; останите унутар.
(*Poh-sleh-dee-tseh zem-lyoh-treh-sah; oh-stah-nee-teh oo-noo-tahr.*)

427. Severe thunderstorm; seek shelter.
Јако невреме; потражите склониште.
(*Yah-koh neh-vreh-meh; poh-trah-zhee-teh skloh-neesh-teh.*)

Emergency Services Information

428. What's the emergency hotline number?
Који је број хитне помоћи?
(Koy-ee yeh broy heet-neh poh-moch-ee?)

429. Where's the nearest police station?
Где је најближа полицијска станица?
(Gdeh yeh nigh-blee-zhah poh-lee-tsee-y-skah stah-nee-tsah?)

430. How do I contact the fire department?
Како да контактирам ватрогасну службу?
(Kah-koh dah kohn-tahk-tee-rahm vah-troh-gahs-noo sloozh-boo?)

431. Is there a hospital nearby?
Да ли има болница у близини?
(Dah lee ee-mah bohl-nee-tsah oo bleeh-zee-nee?)

432. What's the number for poison control?
Који је број за контролу тровања?
(Koy-ee yeh broy zah kohn-troh-loo troh-vah-nyah?)

433. Where can I find a disaster relief center?
Где могу наћи центар за помоћ у случају катастрофе?
(Gdeh moh-goo nah-chee tsehn-tahr zah poh-moch oo sloo-chigh-yoo kah-tah-stroh-feh?)

> **Fun Fact:** Serbian is known for complex tongue twisters that are fun to try.

434. What's the local emergency radio station?
Која је локална хитна радио станица?
(*Koy-ya yeh loh-kahl-nah heet-nah rah-dee-oh stah-nee-tsah?*)

435. Are there any shelters in the area?
Има ли склоништа у подручју?
(*Ee-mah lee skloh-neesh-tah oo poh-droo-choo?*)

436. Who do I call for road assistance?
Коме да се обратим за помоћ на путу?
(*Koh-meh dah seh oh-brah-teem zah poh-moch nah poo-too?*)

437. How can I reach search and rescue teams?
Како могу да контактирам тимове за тражење и спасавање?
(*Kah-koh moh-goo dah kohn-tahk-tee-rahm tee-moh-veh zah trah-zheh-nyeh ee spah-sah-vah-nyeh?*)

> "Свака птица своме јату лети."
> **"Every bird flies to its flock."**
> *People are drawn to those
> similar to themselves.*

100

Interactive Challenge: Emergencies Quiz

1. **How do you say "emergency" in Serbian?**

   a) Јабука
   b) Хитан случај
   c) Сир
   d) Плажа

2. **What's the Serbian word for "ambulance"?**

   a) Аутомобил
   b) Бицикл
   c) Хитна помоћ
   d) Школа

3. **If you need immediate medical attention, what should you say in Serbian?**

   a) Желим хлеб.
   b) Где је станица?
   c) Треба ми хитна медицинска помоћ.

4. **How do you ask "Is there a hospital nearby?" in Serbian?**

   a) Где је биоскоп?
   b) Имате ли оловку?
   c) Има ли болница у близини?

5. **What's the Serbian word for "police"?**

   a) Јабука
   b) Полиција
   c) Воз

6. **How do you say "fire" in Serbian?**

   a) Сунце
   b) Пас
   c) Пожар
   d) Књига

7. **If you've witnessed an accident, what phrase can you use in Serbian?**

   a) Желим чоколаду.
   b) Видео сам несрећу.
   c) Волим цвеће.
   d) Ово је моја кућа.

8. **What's the Serbian word for "help"?**

   a) Довиђења
   b) Добар дан
   c) Хвала
   d) У помоћ!

9. **How would you say "I've been robbed; I need the authorities" in Serbian?**

   a) Јео сам сир.
   b) Опљачкан сам; требају ми власти.
   c) Ово је лепа планина.

10. **How do you ask "Can you call an ambulance, please?" in Serbian?**

    a) Можете ли позвати такси, молим?
    b) Можете ли ми дати со?
    c) Можете ли позвати хитну помоћ, молим?

11. What's the Serbian word for "emergency services"?

    a) Хитне службе
    b) Укусна торта
    c) Лагано

12. How do you say "reporting an accident" in Serbian?

    a) Певати песму
    b) Читати књигу
    c) Пријавити несрећу

13. If you need to contact the fire department, what should you say in Serbian?

    a) Како да дођем до библиотеке?
    b) Морам контактирати ватрогасце.
    c) Тражим пријатеља.

14. What's the Serbian word for "urgent"?

    a) Мали
    b) Леп
    c) Брз
    d) Хитно

15. How do you ask for the nearest police station in Serbian?

    a) Где је најближа пекара?
    b) Где је најближа полицијска станица?
    c) Имате ли мапу?
    d) Колико је сати?

Correct Answers:

1. b)
2. c)
3. c)
4. c)
5. b)
6. c)
7. b)
8. d)
9. b)
10. c)
11. a)
12. c)
13. b)
14. d)
15. b)

EVERYDAY CONVERSATIONS

- SMALL TALK AND CASUAL CONVERSATIONS -
- DISCUSSING THE WEATHER, HOBBIES, AND INTERESTS -
- MAKING PLANS WITH FRIENDS OR ACQUAINTANCES -

Small Talk

438.   How's it going?
Како идеш?
(*Kah-koh ee-desh?*)

439.   Nice weather we're having, isn't it?
Лепо време, зар не?
(*Leh-poh vreh-meh, zar neh?*)

440.   Have any exciting plans for the weekend?
Имате ли узбудљиве планове за викенд?
(*Ee-mah-teh lee ooz-boo-dlyee-veh plah-no-veh zah vee-kend?*)

441.   Did you catch that new movie?
Да ли сте гледали тај нови филм?
(*Dah lee steh gleh-dah-lee tie noh-vee feelm?*)

442.   How's your day been so far?
Како вам је протекао дан до сада?
(*Kah-koh vahm yeh proh-teh-kah-oh dahn doh sah-dah?*)

443.   What do you do for work?
Чиме се бавите?
(*Chee-meh seh bah-vee-teh?*)

444.   Do you come here often?
Да ли често долазите овде?
(*Dah lee chehs-toh doh-lah-zee-teh ohv-deh?*)

445.   Have you tried the food at this place before?
Да ли сте раније пробали храну овде?
(*Dah lee steh rah-nee-yeh proh-bah-lee khrah-noo ohv-deh?*)

446. Any recommendations for things to do in town?
Имате ли препоруке за ствари које може да се ради у граду?
(*Ee-mah-teh lee preh-poh-roo-keh zah stvah-ree koh-yeh moh-zheh dah seh rah-dee oo grah-doo?*)

447. Do you follow any sports teams?
Пратите ли неки спортски тим?
(*Prah-tee-teh lee neh-kee spohrt-skee teem?*)

448. Have you traveled anywhere interesting lately?
Да ли сте недавно путовали негде занимљиво?
(*Dah lee steh neh-dahv-noh poo-toh-vah-lee neh-gdeh zah-neem-lyee-voh?*)

449. Do you enjoy cooking?
Да ли уживате у кувању?
(*Dah lee oo-zhee-vah-teh oo koo-vah-nyoo?*)

> **Travel Story:** In a bustling café in Niš, a group of friends described their lively discussion as, "Разговор за милион долара," translating to "A million-dollar conversation."

Casual Conversations

450. What's your favorite type of music?
Који је ваш омиљени музички жанр?
(*Koh-yee yeh vahsh oh-mee-lyeh-nee moo-zeech-kee zhanr?*)

> **Fun Fact:** Serbian is often used in love songs and ballads.

451. How do you like to spend your free time?
Како волите да проводите слободно време?
(*Kah-koh voh-lee-teh dah proh-voh-dee-teh sloh-bohd-noh vreh-meh?*)

452. Do you have any pets?
Имате ли кућне љубимце?
(*Ee-mah-teh lee kooch-neh lyoo-beem-tseh?*)

453. Where did you grow up?
Где сте одрасли?
(*Gdeh steh oh-drah-slee?*)

454. What's your family like?
Каква вам је породица?
(*Kah-kvah vahm yeh poh-roh-dee-tsah?*)

455. Are you a morning person or a night owl?
Да ли сте јутарњи тип или ноћна сова?
(*Dah lee steh yoo-tahr-nyee teep ee-lee nohch-nah soh-vah?*)

456. Do you prefer coffee or tea?
Да ли више волите кафу или чај?
(*Dah lee vee-sheh voh-lee-teh kah-foo ee-lee chai?*)

457. Are you into any TV shows right now?
Гледате ли тренутно неку ТВ серију?
(*Gleh-dah-teh lee treh-noot-noh neh-koo TV se-ree-yoo?*)

> **Idiomatic Expression:** "Бити добар као хлеб." -
> Meaning: "To be a very good person."
> (Literal translation: "To be as good as bread.")

458. What's the last book you read?
Која је последња књига коју сте прочитали?
(*Koy-yah yeh poh-sled-nyah k-nyee-gah koy-yoo steh proh-chee-tah-lee?*)

459. Do you like to travel?
Волите ли да путујете?
(*Voh-lee-teh lee dah poot-oo-yeh-teh?*)

460. Are you a fan of outdoor activities?
Волите ли активности на отвореном?
(*Voh-lee-teh lee ak-tee-vnohs-tee nah ot-voh-reh-nohm?*)

461. How do you unwind after a long day?
Како се опуштате након дугог дана?
(*Kah-koh seh oh-poosh-tah-teh nah-kohn doo-gohg dah-nah?*)

Discussing the Weather

462. Can you believe this heat/cold?
Можете ли веровати у ову врућину/хладноћу?
(*Moh-zheh-teh lee veh-roh-vah-tee oo oh-voo vroo-chee-noo/kh lad-noh-choo?*)

463. I heard it's going to rain all week.
Чуо/ла сам да ће целе недеље падати киша.
(*Choo-oh/lah sahm dah cheh tseh-leh neh-deh-lyeh pah-dah-tee kee-shah.*)

464. What's the temperature like today?
Каква је данас температура?
(*Kah-kvah yeh dah-nahs tehm-peh-rah-too-rah?*)

465. Do you like sunny or cloudy days better?
Да ли више волите сунчане или облачне дане?
(*Dah lee vee-sheh voh-lee-teh soon-chah-neh ee-lee ob-lahch-neh dah-neh?*)

466. Have you ever seen a snowstorm like this?
Да ли сте икада видели овакву снежну олују?
(*Dah lee steh ee-kah-dah vee-deh-lee oh-vah-kvoo snezh-noo oh-loo-yoo?*)

467. Is it always this humid here?
Да ли је увек овако влажно овде?
(*Dah lee yeh oo-vek oh-vah-koh vlahzh-noh ohv-deh?*)

468. Did you get caught in that thunderstorm yesterday?
Да ли сте били ухваћени у јучерашњој грмљавини?
(*Dah lee steh bee-lee ooh-khvah-cheh-nee oo yoo-cheh-rahsh-nyoy grm-lya-vee-nee?*)

469. What's the weather like in your hometown?
Какво је време у вашем родном граду?
(*Kahk-voh yeh vreh-meh oo vah-shem rohd-nohm grah-doo?*)

470. I can't stand the wind; how about you?
Не могу да поднесем ветар; а ви?
(*Neh moh-goo dah poh-dneh-sehm veh-tahr; ah vee?*)

471. Is it true the winters here are mild?
Да ли је тачно да су зиме овде благе?
(*Dah lee yeh tach-noh dah soo zee-meh ohv-deh blah-geh?*)

472. Do you like beach weather?
Да ли волите време за плажу?
(*Dah lee voh-lee-teh vreh-meh zah plah-zhoo?*)

473. How do you cope with the humidity in summer?
Како се носите са влажношћу током лета?
(*Kah-koh seh noh-see-teh sah vlahzh-nosh-choo toh-kohm leh-tah?*)

Hobbies

474. What are your hobbies or interests?
Који су ваши хобији или интереси?
(*Koy-ee soo vah-shee hoh-bee-yee ee-lee een-teh-reh-see?*)

475. Do you play any musical instruments?
Да ли свирате неки музички инструмент?
(*Dah lee svee-rah-teh neh-kee moo-zeech-kee een-stroo-ment?*)

476. Have you ever tried painting or drawing?
Да ли сте икада пробали сликање или цртање?
(*Dah lee steh ee-kah-dah proh-bah-lee slee-kah-nyeh ee-lee tsrt-ah-nyeh?*)

477. Are you a fan of sports?
Да ли сте љубитељ спорта?
(*Dah lee steh lyoo-bee-tehl spohr-tah?*)

478. Do you enjoy cooking or baking?
Да ли уживате у кувању или печењу?
(*Dah lee oo-zhee-vah-teh oo koo-vah-nyoo ee-lee peh-cheh-nyoo?*)

479. Are you into photography?
Да ли вас занима фотографија?
(*Dah lee vahs zah-nee-mah foh-toh-grah-fee-yah?*)

480. Have you ever tried gardening?
Да ли сте икада покушали баштованство?
(*Dah lee steh ee-kah-dah poh-koo-shah-lee bash-toh-vahn-stvoh?*)

481. Do you like to read in your free time?
Да ли волите да читате у слободно време?
(*Dah lee voh-lee-teh dah chee-tah-teh oo sloh-bohd-noh vreh-meh?*)

482. Have you explored any new hobbies lately?
Да ли сте у последње време истраживали нове хобије?
(*Dah lee steh oo pohs-lehd-nyeh vreh-meh ees-trah-zhee-vah-lee noh-veh hoh-bee-ye?*)

483. Are you a collector of anything?
Да ли сте колекционар нечега?
(*Dah lee steh koh-lehk-tsyoh-nahr neh-cheh-gah?*)

484. Do you like to watch movies or TV shows?
Да ли волите да гледате филмове или ТВ емисије?
(*Dah lee voh-lee-teh dah gleh-dah-teh feel-moh-veh ee-lee TV eh-mee-si-ye?*)

485. Have you ever taken up a craft project?
Да ли сте икада започели занатски пројекат?
(*Dah lee steh ee-kah-dah zah-poh-cheh-lee zah-naht-skee proh-yeh-kaht?*)

> **Idiomatic Expression:** "Правити се луд." -
> Meaning: "To play dumb."
> (Literal translation: "To make oneself crazy.")

Interests

486. What topics are you passionate about?
За које теме сте страствени?
(Zah koh-yeh teh-meh steh strah-stveh-nee?)

487. Are you involved in any social causes?
Да ли сте укључени у неке друштвене акције?
(Dah lee steh ooh-klyoo-cheh-nee oo neh-keh droosh-tveh-neh ahk-tsee-ye?)

488. Do you enjoy learning new languages?
Да ли уживате у учењу нових језика?
(Dah lee oo-zhee-vah-teh oo oo-cheh-nyoo noh-veeh yeh-zee-kah?)

489. Are you into fitness or wellness?
Да ли сте заинтересовани за фитнес или велнес?
(Dah lee steh zah-een-teh-reh-soh-vah-nee zah feet-nes ee-lee vehl-nes?)

490. Are you a technology enthusiast?
Да ли сте ентузијаста за технологију?
(Dah lee steh en-too-zee-yah-stah zah teh-hnoh-loh-gee-yoo?)

491. What's your favorite genre of books or movies?
Који је ваш омиљени жанр књига или филмова?
(Koh-yee yeh vahsh oh-mee-lyeh-nee zhanr knyee-gah ee-lee feel-moh-vah?)

492. Do you follow current events or politics?
Да ли пратите актуелна дешавања или политику?
(Dah lee prah-tee-teh ahk-too-ehl-nah deh-shah-vah-nyah ee-lee poh-lee-tee-koo?)

493. Are you into fashion or design?
Да ли вас занима мода или дизајн?
(Dah lee vahs zah-nee-mah moh-dah ee-lee dee-zighn?)

494. Are you a history buff?
Да ли сте љубитељ историје?
(Dah lee steh lyoo-bee-tehlj ees-toh-ree-ye?)

495. Have you ever been involved in volunteer work?
Да ли сте икада учествовали у волонтерском раду?
(Dah lee steh ee-kah-dah oo-chest-vo-vah-lee oo vo-lon-tehr-skohm rah-doo?)

496. Are you passionate about cooking or food culture?
Да ли сте страствени око кувања или кулинарске културе?
(Dah lee steh strah-stveh-nee oh-koh koo-vah-nyah ee-lee koo-lee-nahr-skeh kool-too-reh?)

497. Are you an advocate for any specific hobbies or interests?
Да ли подржавате неке специфичне хобије или интересе?
(Dah lee poh-dzha-vah-teh neh-keh speh-tsee-fee-chneh hoh-bee-ye ee-lee een-teh-reh-seh?)

> **Idiomatic Expression:** "Изаћи на зелену грану." -
> Meaning: "To succeed in life."
> (Literal translation: "To come out on a green branch.")

Making Plans

498. Would you like to grab a coffee sometime?
Да ли бисте желели да попијемо кафу некад?
(Dah lee bees-teh zheh-leh-lee dah poh-pee-yeh-moh kah-foo neh-kahd?)

499. Let's plan a dinner outing this weekend.
Хајде да планирамо вечеру овог викенда.
(*Hay-deh dah plah-nee-rah-moh veh-cheh-roo oh-vog vee-kehn-dah.*)

500. How about going to a movie on Friday night?
Шта кажете на филм у петак увече?
(*Shta kah-zheh-teh nah feelm oo peh-tahk oo-veh-cheh?*)

501. Do you want to join us for a hike next weekend?
Да ли желите да нам се придружите на планинарењу следећег викенда?
(*Dah lee zheh-lee-teh dah nahm seh pree-droo-zhee-teh nah plah-nee-nah-reh-nyoo sleh-deh-chehg vee-kehn-dah?*)

502. We should organize a game night soon.
Требало би да организујемо играчку вече ускоро.
(*Treh-bah-loh bee dah or-gah-nee-zoo-yeh-moh eeg-rah-choo-keh veh-cheh oo-skoh-roh.*)

503. Let's catch up over lunch next week.
Хајде да се видимо на ручку следеће недеље.
(*Hay-deh dah seh vee-dee-moh nah rooch-koo sleh-deh-cheh neh-deh-lyeh.*)

504. Would you be interested in a shopping trip?
Да ли бисте били заинтересовани за шопинг?
(*Dah lee bees-teh bee-lee zah-een-teh-reh-soh-vah-nee zah shop-eeng?*)

505. I'm thinking of visiting the museum; care to join?
Размишљам да посетим музеј; да ли желите да се придружите?
(*Rahz-mee-shlyahm dah poh-seh-teem moo-zay; dah lee zheh-lee-teh dah seh pree-droo-zhee-teh?*)

506. How about a picnic in the park?
Шта кажеш на пикник у парку?
(*Shta kah-zhesh nah peek-neek oo par-koo?*)

> **Fun Fact:** Serbian has interesting palindromes like "potop" (flood) and "kobajagi" (pretend).

507. Let's get together for a study session.
Хајде да се окупимо за учење.
(*Hay-deh dah seh oh-koo-pee-moh zah oo-cheh-nyeh.*)

508. We should plan a beach day this summer.
Требало би да планирамо дан на плажи овог лета.
(*Treh-bah-loh bee dah plah-nee-rah-moh dahn nah plah-zhee oh-vog leh-tah.*)

509. Want to come over for a barbecue at my place?
Желиш ли да дођеш на роштиљ код мене?
(*Zheh-leesh lee dah doh-jesh nah rosh-teelj kod meh-neh?*)

> "Пас који лаје не једа."
> **"A barking dog doesn't bite."**
> *People who make the loudest threats often do not act on them.*

116

Interactive Challenge: Everyday Conversations
(Link each English word with their corresponding meaning in Serbian)

1) Conversation	Размена мишљења
2) Greeting	Ћаскање
3) Question	Питање
4) Answer	Поздрав
5) Salutation	Дељење идеја
6) Communication	Разговор
7) Dialogue	Комуникација
8) Small Talk	Говор
9) Discussion	Одговор
10) Speech	Језик
11) Language	Дискусија
12) Exchange of Opinions	Необавезан разговор
13) Expression	Поздрављање
14) Casual Conversation	Дијалог
15) Sharing Ideas	Израз

Correct Answers:

1. Conversation - Разговор
2. Greeting - Поздрав
3. Question - Питање
4. Answer - Одговор
5. Salutation - Поздрављање
6. Communication - Комуникација
7. Dialogue - Дијалог
8. Small Talk - Ћаскање
9. Discussion - Дискусија
10. Speech - Говор
11. Language - Језик
12. Exchange of Opinions - Размена мишљења
13. Expression - Израз
14. Casual Conversation - Необавезан разговор
15. Sharing Ideas - Дељење идеја

BUSINESS & WORK

- INTRODUCING YOURSELF IN A PROFESSIONAL SETTING -
- DISCUSSING WORK-RELATED TOPICS -
- NEGOTIATING BUSINESS DEALS OR CONTRACTS -

Professional Introductions

510. Hi, I'm [Your Name].
     Здраво, ја сам [Ваше Име].
     (Zdrah-vo, ya sam [Vah-sheh Ee-meh].)

511. What do you do for a living?
     Чиме се бавите?
     (Chee-meh seh bah-vee-teh?)

512. What's your role in the company?
     Која је Ваша позиција у компанији?
     (Koh-yah yeh Vah-shah poh-zee-tsee-yah oo kom-pan-ee-yee?)

513. Can you tell me about your background?
     Можете ли ми рећи нешто о свом образовању?
     (Moh-zheh-teh lee mee reh-chee neh-shtoh oh svom oh-brah-zoh-vah-nyoo?)

514. This is my colleague, [Colleague's Name].
     Ово је мој колега, [Име Колеге].
     (O-voh yeh moy koh-leh-gah, [Ee-meh Koh-leh-geh].)

515. May I introduce myself?
     Могу ли да се представим?
     (Moh-goo lee dah seh prehd-stah-veem?)

516. I work in [Your Department].
     Радим у [Вашем Одељењу].
     (Rah-deem oo [Vah-shehm Oh-delye-nyoo].)

517. How long have you been with the company?
     Колико дуго сте у компанији?
     (Koh-lee-koh doo-goh steh oo kom-pan-ee-yee?)

518.   Are you familiar with our team?
Да ли сте упознати са нашим тимом?
(Dah lee steh oo-pohz-nah-tee sah nah-sheem tee-mohm?)

519.   Let me introduce you to our manager.
Дозволите ми да Вас упознам са нашим менаџером.
(Dohz-voh-lee-teh mee dah Vas oo-pohz-nahm sah nah-sheem meh-nah-jeh-rohm.)

> **Travel Story:** While tasting ajvar (pepper spread) at a local market, a tourist said, "Ово је прави укус Србије," meaning "This is the true taste of Serbia."

Work Conversations

520.   Can we discuss the project?
Можемо ли да разговарамо о пројекту?
(Moh-zheh-moh lee dah rahz-goh-vah-rah-moh oh proh-yehk-too?)

521.   Let's go over the details.
Хајде да прегледамо детаље.
(Hay-deh dah preh-gleh-dah-moh deh-tahl-yeh.)

522.   What's the agenda for the meeting?
Какав је дневни ред за састанак?
(Kah-kahv yeh dnehv-nee red zah sah-stah-nahk?)

523.   I'd like your input on this.
Волео бих да чујем Ваше мишљење о овоме.
(Voh-leh-oh bih dah choo-yem Vah-sheh meesh-lyeh-nyeh oh oh-voh-meh.)

524. We need to address this issue.
Треба да се бавимо овим проблемом.
(Treh-bah dah seh bah-vee-moh oh-veem proh-bleh-mohm.)

525. How's the project progressing?
Како напредује пројекат?
(Kah-koh nah-preh-doo-yeh proh-yek-aht?)

526. Do you have any updates for me?
Имате ли неке новости за мене?
(Ee-mah-teh lee neh-keh noh-vo-stee zah meh-neh?)

527. Let's brainstorm some ideas.
Хајде да скупимо идеје.
(Hay-deh dah skoo-peemoh ee-deh-yeh.)

528. Can we schedule a team meeting?
Можемо ли заказати тимски састанак?
(Moh-zhem lee zah-kah-zahtee teem-skee sahs-tah-nahk?)

529. I'm open to suggestions.
Отворен сам за предлоге.
(Oht-voh-ren sahm zah preh-dloh-geh.)

Business Negotiations

530. We need to negotiate the terms.
Треба да преговарамо о условима.
(Treh-bah dah preh-goh-vah-rah-moh oh oos-loh-vee-mah.)

531. What's your offer?
Шта предлажете?
(*Shtah preh-dlah-zheh-teh?*)

532. Can we find a middle ground?
Можемо ли пронаћи средину?
(*Moh-zhem lee proh-nah-chi sreh-dee-noo?*)

> **Idiomatic Expression:** "Ко последњи, њему две." -
> Meaning: "The last one gets a double portion."
> (Literal translation: "Whoever is last, gets two.")

533. Let's discuss the contract.
Хајде да разговарамо о уговору.
(*Hay-deh dah rahz-goh-vah-rah-moh oh oo-goh-voh-roo.*)

534. Are you flexible on the price?
Јесте ли флексибилни по питању цене?
(*Yes-teh lee flehk-see-beel-nee poh pee-tah-nyoo tseh-neh?*)

535. I'd like to propose a deal.
Желим да предложим посао.
(*Zheh-leem dah preh-dloh-zheem poh-sah-oh.*)

536. We're interested in your terms.
Заинтересовани смо за ваше услове.
(*Zah-eeh-nteh-reh-soo-vaht nee vah-shee-teh oos-loh-veh.*)

537. Can we talk about the agreement?
Можемо ли причати о споразуму?
(*Moh-zhem lee pree-chahtee oh spo-rah-zoo-moo?*)

> **Fun Fact:** Serbia has produced renowned athletes,
> especially in tennis and basketball.

538.   Let's work out the details.
Хајде да утврдимо детаље.
(*Hay-deh dah oot-vrdee-moh deh-tal-ye.*)

539.   What are your conditions?
Какви су ваши услови?
(*Kahk-vee soo vah-shee oo-sloh-vee?*)

540.   We should reach a compromise.
Треба да постигнемо компромис.
(*Tre-bah dah pohs-tee-gneh-moh kom-proh-mees.*)

> **Fun Fact:** Orthodox Christianity is a significant aspect of Serbian culture and heritage.

Workplace Etiquette

541.   Remember to be punctual.
Запамтите да будете тачни.
(*Zah-pahm-tee-teh dah boo-deh-teh tahch-nee.*)

542.   Always maintain a professional demeanor.
Увек одржавајте професионалан став.
(*Oo-vek o-druh-zhah-vahy-teh proh-feh-see-oh-nah-lahn stahv.*)

543.   Respect your colleagues' personal space.
Поштујте лични простор колега.
(*Poh-shtoo-yteh leech-nee proh-stohr koh-leh-gah.*)

> **Fun Fact:** Serbian cuisine is known for dishes like ćevapi, sarma, and ajvar.

544. Dress appropriately for the office.
Облачите се прикладно за канцеларију.
(*Oh-blah-chee-teh seh pree-klahd-noh zah kahn-tseh-lah-ree-yoo.*)

545. Follow company policies and guidelines.
Пратите политике и смернице компаније.
(*Prah-tee-teh poh-lee-tee-keh ee smehr-nee-tseh kohm-pah-nee-ye.*)

546. Use respectful language in conversations.
Користите учтив језик у разговорима.
(*Koh-rees-tee-teh ooch-teev yeh-zihk oo rahz-goh-voh-ree-mah.*)

547. Keep your workspace organized.
Организујте свој радни простор.
(*Or-gah-nee-zooy-teh svoy rahd-nee proh-stohr.*)

548. Be mindful of office noise levels.
Будите свесни нивоа буке у канцеларији.
(*Boo-dee-teh svehs-nee nee-voh-ah boo-keh oo kahn-tseh-lah-ree-yee.*)

549. Offer assistance when needed.
Понудите помоћ када је потребно.
(*Poh-noo-dee-teh poh-moch kah-dah yeh poh-trehb-noh.*)

550. Practice good hygiene at work.
Одржавајте добру хигијену на посао.
(*O-druh-zhah-vahy-teh doh-broo hee-ghee-ye-noo nah poh-sah-oh.*)

551. Avoid office gossip and rumors.
Избегавајте трачеве и гласине у канцеларији.
(*Eez-beh-gah-vahy-teh trah-cheh-veh ee glah-see-neh oo kahn-tseh-lah-ree-yee.*)

Job Interviews

552. Tell me about yourself.
      Реците ми нешто о себи.
      (*Reh-tsee-teh mee neh-shtoh o seh-bee.*)

553. What are your strengths and weaknesses?
      Које су ваше снаге и слабости?
      (*Koyeh soo vah-sheh snah-geh ee slah-bohs-tee?*)

554. Describe your relevant experience.
      Опишите ваше релевантно искуство.
      (*Oh-pee-shee-teh vah-sheh reh-leh-vahnt-noh ees-koos-tvoh.*)

555. Why do you want to work here?
      Зашто желите да радите овде?
      (*Zah-shtoh zheh-lee-teh dah rah-dee-teh ohv-deh?*)

556. Where do you see yourself in five years?
      Где се видите за пет година?
      (*Gdeh seh vee-dee-teh zah peht goh-dee-nah?*)

557. How do you handle challenges at work?
      Како се носите с изазовима на посао?
      (*Kah-koh seh noh-see-teh s ee-zah-zoh-vee-mah nah poh-sah-oh?*)

558. What interests you about this position?
      Шта вас привлачи на овој позицији?
      (*Shta vahs preev-lah-chee nah oh-voy poh-zee-tsyee?*)

559. Can you provide an example of your teamwork?
Можете ли дати пример ваше тимске раде?
(*Moh-zheh-teh lee dah-tee pree-mehr vah-sheh teem-skeh rah-deh?*)

560. What motivates you in your career?
Шта вас мотивише у вашој каријери?
(*Shta vahs moh-tee-vih-sheh oo vah-shoy kah-ree-yeh-ree?*)

561. Do you have any questions for us?
Имате ли нека питања за нас?
(*Ee-mah-teh lee neh-kah pee-tahn-yah zah nahs?*)

562. Thank you for considering me for the role.
Хвала што сте ме разматрали за ову улогу.
(*Khvah-lah shtoh steh meh rahz-mah-trah-lee zah oh-voo oo-loh-goo.*)

Office Communication

563. Send me an email about it.
Пошаљте ми имејл о томе.
(*Poh-shahl-nyeh-tee mee eeh-mayl oh toh-meh.*)

564. Let's schedule a conference call.
Да закажемо конференцијски позив.
(*Dah zah-kah-zeh-moh kohn-feh-rehn-tsyee-skee poh-zeev.*)

565. Could you clarify your message?
Можете ли појаснити вашу поруку?
(*Moh-zheh-teh lee poy-ahs-nee-tee vah-shoo poh-roo-koo?*)

566.   I'll forward the document to you.
Проследићу вам документ.
(*Pro-sleh-dee-tchoo vahm doh-koo-ment.*)

567.   Please reply to this message.
Молим вас, одговорите на ову поруку.
(*Moh-leem vahs, od-goh-voh-ree-teh nah oh-voo poh-roo-koo.*)

568.   We should have a team meeting.
Треба да имамо тимски састанак.
(*Tre-bah dah ee-mah-moh teem-skee sah-stah-nahk.*)

> **Idiomatic Expression:** "Не бити свој." -
> Meaning: "To feel not like oneself."
> (Literal translation: "To not be one's own.")

569.   Check your inbox for updates.
Проверите свој инбокс за ажурирања.
(*Proh-veh-ree-teh svoy in-boks zah ah-zhoo-ree-rah-nyah.*)

570.   I'll copy you on the correspondence.
Укључићу вас у кореспонденцију.
(*Oo-klyoo-chee-tchoo vahs oo koh-reh-spon-den-tsyee-yoo.*)

571.   I'll send you the meeting agenda.
Послаћу вам дневни ред састанка.
(*Poh-slah-tchoo vahm dnev-nee red sah-stahn-kah.*)

572.   Use the internal messaging system.
Користите интерни систем за поруке.
(*Koh-rees-tee-teh een-tehr-nee sis-tehm zah poh-roo-keh.*)

573.   Keep everyone in the loop.
         Обавештавајте све о сваком новом развоју.
         (*Oh-bah-vesh-tah-vahy-teh sveh o svah-kohm noh-vohm
         rahz-voh-yoo.*)

> "Једна ласта не чини пролеће."
> **"One swallow does not make a spring."**
> *A single positive event does not mean
> that what follows will be good.*

Cross Word Puzzle: Business & Work

(Provide the Serbian translation for the following English words)

Across

3. - INCOME
5. - CONTRACT
6. - PROJECT
11. - SALARY
12. - BOSS
13. - CLIENT
14. - BUSINESS

Down

1. - PRODUCT
2. - SERVICE
4. - PROFESSIONAL
6. - WORK
7. - OFFICE
8. - TEAM
9. - EMPLOYEE
10. - MARKETING

Correct Answers:

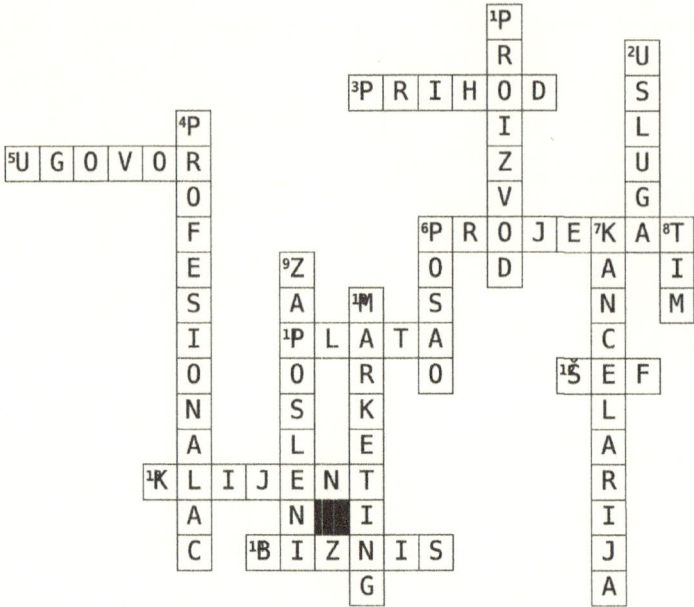

EVENTS & ENTERTAINMENT

- BUYING TICKETS FOR CONCERTS, MOVIES OR EVENTS -
- DISCUSSING ENTERTAINMENT & LEISURE ACTIVITIES -
- EXPRESSING JOY OR DISAPPOINTMENT WITH AN EVENT -

Ticket Purchases

574.   I'd like to buy two tickets for the concert.
        Желим да купим две карте за концерт.
        (*Zheh-leem dah koo-peem dveh kar-teh zah kon-tsehrt.*)

575.   Can I get tickets for the movie tonight?
        Могу ли да купим карте за вечерашњи филм?
        (*Moh-goo lee dah koo-peem kar-teh zah veh-cheh-rash-njee feelm?*)

576.   We need to book tickets for the upcoming event.
        Треба да резервишемо карте за предстојећи догађај.
        (*Tre-bah dah reh-zer-vee-sheh-moh kar-teh zah prehd-stoy-eh-tchee doh-gah-djai.*)

577.   What's the price of admission?
        Колика је цена улаза?
        (*Koh-lee-kah yeh tseh-nah oo-lah-zah?*)

578.   Do you offer any discounts for students?
        Да ли имате попусте за студенте?
        (*Dah lee ee-mah-teh poh-poos-teh zah stoo-dehn-teh?*)

579.   Are there any available seats for the matinee?
        Да ли има слободних места за матине?
        (*Dah lee ee-mah sloh-bohd-neeh meh-stah zah mah-tee-neh?*)

580.   How can I purchase tickets online?
        Како могу да купим карте преко интернета?
        (*Kah-koh moh-goo dah koo-peem kar-teh preh-koh een-tehr-neh-tah?*)

581. Is there a box office nearby?
Да ли је близу благајна?
(*Dah lee yeh bleeh-zoo blah-gah-ee-nah?*)

582. Are tickets refundable if I can't attend?
Да ли се карте могу вратити ако не могу да присуствујем?
(*Dah lee seh kar-teh moh-goo vrah-tee-tee ah-koh neh moh-goo dah pree-soos-too-yehm?*)

583. Can I choose my seats for the show?
Могу ли да изаберем своја места за представу?
(*Moh-goo lee dah ee-zah-beh-rem svoy-ah meh-stah zah prehd-stah-voo?*)

584. Can I reserve tickets for the theater?
Могу ли да резервишем карте за позориште?
(*Moh-goo lee dah reh-zer-vee-shehm kar-teh zah poh-zoh-reesh-teh?*)

585. How early should I buy event tickets?
Колико рано треба да купим карте за догађај?
(*Koh-lee-koh rah-noh tre-bah dah koo-peem kar-teh zah doh-gah-djai?*)

586. Are there any VIP packages available?
Да ли има доступних VIP пакета?
(*Dah lee ee-mah doh-stoo-pneeh Vee-ee-peh pah-keh-tah?*)

587. What's the seating arrangement like?
Какав је распоред седења?
(*Kah-kahv yeh rah-spo-rehd seh-dye-nyah?*)

> **Idiomatic Expression:** "Немати длаке на језику." -
> Meaning: "To speak one's mind."
> (Literal translation: "To have no hair on one's tongue.")

588. Is there a family discount for the movie?
Да ли има породични попуст за филм?
(*Dah lee ee-mah po-roh-deech-nee po-poost zah feelm?*)

589. I'd like to purchase tickets for my friends.
Желим да купим карте за моје пријатеље.
(*Zheh-leem dah koo-peem kar-teh zah moy-eh pree-ya-te-lyeh.*)

> **Fun Fact:** Serbian nouns and adjectives are gender-specific.

590. Do they accept credit cards for tickets?
Да ли се примају кредитне картице за карте?
(*Dah lee seh pree-ma-yoo kre-deet-neh kar-tee-tseh zah kar-teh?*)

591. Are there any age restrictions for entry?
Да ли има старосних ограничења за улаз?
(*Dah lee ee-mah stah-rohs-neeh oh-grah-nee-chehn-ya zah oo-lahz?*)

592. Can I exchange my ticket for a different date?
Могу ли да заменим картицу за други датум?
(*Moh-goo lee dah zah-meh-neem kar-tee-tsoo zah droo-ghee dah-toom?*)

Leisure Activities

593. What do you feel like doing this weekend?
Шта желиш да радимо овог викенда?
(*Shta zheh-lish dah rah-dee-moh oh-vogh vee-kehndah?*)

594. Let's discuss our entertainment options.
Хајде да разговарамо о нашим опцијама за забаву.
(*Haj-deh dah raz-goh-vah-rah-moh o nah-sheem op-tsee-yah-mah zah zah-bah-voo.*)

> **Fun Fact:** German, Hungarian, and Russian have influenced Serbian.

595. I'm planning a leisurely hike on Saturday.
Планирам опуштену шетњу у суботу.
(*Plah-nee-rahm oh-poosh-teh-noo sheh-nyoo oo soo-boh-too.*)

596. Do you enjoy outdoor activities like hiking?
Да ли уживаш у активностима на отвореном као што је планинарење?
(*Dah lee oo-zhee-vahsh oo ak-teev-noh-stee-mah nah oht-voh-reh-nohm kah-oh shtoh yeh plah-nee-nah-reh-nyeh?*)

597. Have you ever tried indoor rock climbing?
Да ли си икада пробао унутрашње пењање по стенама?
(*Dah lee see ee-kah-dah proh-bah-oh oo-noo-trahsh-nyeh peh-nyah-nyeh poh steh-nah-mah?*)

598. I'd like to explore some new hobbies.
Желим да истражим неке нове хобије.
(*Zheh-leem dah ees-trah-zheem neh-keh noh-veh ho-bee-ye.*)

599. What are your favorite pastimes?
Који су твоји омиљени начини провођења слободног времена?
(*Koy-ee soo tvoy-ee oh-mee-lyeh-nee nah-chee-nee proh-voh-dye-nyah sloh-bohd-nog vreh-meh-nah?*)

> **Cultural Insight:** Serbian society is very family-oriented, with close-knit family units and frequent family gatherings.

600. Are there any interesting events in town?
Да ли има занимљивих догађаја у граду?
(*Dah lee ee-ma zah-neem-lyee-veeh doh-gah-jah oo grah-doo?*)

601. Let's check out the local art exhibition.
Хајде да погледамо локалну уметничку изложбу.
(*Haj-deh dah poh-gleh-dah-moh loh-kahl-noo oo-met-neech-koo eez-lozh-boo.*)

602. How about attending a cooking class?
Шта мислите о кулинарском курсу?
(*Shta mees-lee-teh o koo-lee-nahr-skohm koor-soo?*)

603. Let's explore some new recreational activities.
Хајде да истражимо нове рекреативне активности.
(*Haj-deh dah ees-trah-zhee-moh no-veh reh-kre-ah-teev-neh ak-teev-nos-tee.*)

604. What's your go-to leisure pursuit?
Која је твоја омиљена активност за слободно време?
(*Koy-ah yeh tvoh-yah oh-mee-lyeh-nah ak-teev-nost zah sloh-bohd-noh vreh-meh?*)

605. I'm considering trying a new hobby.
Размишљам о пробању новог хобија.
(*Raz-meesh-lyahm o proh-bah-nyoo noh-vohg hoh-bee-ya.*)

606. Have you ever attended a painting workshop?
Да ли сте икада присуствовали сликарској радионици?
(*Dah lee steh ee-kah-dah pree-soo-stvoh-vah-lee slee-kahr-skoy ra-dee-oh-nee-tsee?*)

> **Fun Fact:** Serbian has a unique way of forming the future tense.

607. What's your favorite way to unwind?
Како највише волите да се опуштате?
(*Kah-koh nigh-vee-she vo-lee-teh dah seh oh-poosh-tah-teh?*)

608. I'm interested in joining a local club.
Заинтересован сам за придруживање локалном клубу.
(*Zay-een-teh-reh-soh-vahn sahm zah pree-droo-zhee-vah-nyeh loh-kahl-nohm kloo-boo.*)

609. Let's plan a day filled with leisure.
Планирајмо дан испуњен опуштањем.
(*Plah-nee-rahy-moh dahn ees-poon-yen oh-poosh-tah-nyehm.*)

610. Have you ever been to a live comedy show?
Да ли сте икада били на комедији уживо?
(*Dah lee steh ee-kah-dah bee-lee nah koh-meh-dee-yee oo-zhee-voh?*)

611. I'd like to attend a cooking demonstration.
Желео/ла бих да посетим кулинарску демонстрацију.
(*Zheh-leh-oh/lah beeh dah poh-seh-teem koo-lee-nahr-skoo deh-mohn-strah-tsee-yoo.*)

> **Fun Fact:** Serbian has numerous Turkish loanwords due to historical it's Ottoman influence.

Event Reactions

612. That concert was amazing! I loved it!
Тај концерт је био фантастичан! Одушевио/ла ме је!
(*Tahy kon-tsehrt yeh byoh fan-tah-stee-chahn! Oh-doo-sheh-vee-oh/lah meh yeh!*)

139

613. I had such a great time at the movie.
Имала/о сам одлично време на филму.
(*Ee-mah-lah/loh sahm ohd-leech-noh vreh-meh nah feel-moo.*)

614. The event exceeded my expectations.
Догађај је надмашио моја очекивања.
(*Doh-gah-dzhai yeh nahd-mah-shee-oh moh-yah oh-cheh-kee-vah-nyah.*)

615. I was thrilled by the performance.
Представа ме је одушевила.
(*Prehd-stah-vah meh yeh oh-doo-sheh-vee-lah.*)

616. It was an unforgettable experience.
То је било нешто незаборавно.
(*Toh yeh bee-loh neh-shtoh neh-zah-boh-rahv-noh.*)

617. I can't stop thinking about that show.
Не могу да престанем да мислим о тој представи.
(*Neh moh-goo dah preh-stah-nem dah mees-leem oh toy prehd-stah-vee.*)

618. Unfortunately, the event was a letdown.
Нажалост, догађај је био разочаравајућ.
(*Nah-zhah-lohst, doh-gah-dzhai yeh bee-oh rah-zoh-cha-rah-vah-yooch.*)

619. I was disappointed with the movie.
Разочаран/а сам филмом.
(*Rah-zoh-cha-rahn/ah sahm feel-mohm.*)

620. The concert didn't meet my expectations.
Концерт није испунио моја очекивања.
(*Kon-tsehrt nee-yeh ees-poo-nee-oh moh-yah oh-cheh-kee-vah-nyah.*)

621. I expected more from the exhibition.
Од изложбе сам очекивао/ла више.
(Ohd eez-lozh-beh sahm oh-cheh-kee-vah-oh/lah veesheh.)

622. The event left me speechless; it was superb!
Догађај ме је оставио без речи; био је изванредан!
(Doh-gah-dzhai meh yeh oh-stah-vee-oh behz reh-chee; bee-oh yeh eez-vahn-reh-dahn!)

623. I was absolutely thrilled with the performance.
Од представе сам био/ла потпуно одушевљен/а.
(Ohd prehd-stah-veh sahm bee-oh/lah poh-tpoo-noh oh-doo-shehv-lyehn/ah.)

624. The movie was a pleasant surprise.
Филм је био пријатно изненађење.
(Feelm yeh bee-oh pree-yaht-noh eez-neh-nah-dzheh-nyeh.)

625. I had such a blast at the exhibition.
Изложба ми је пружила фантастичан доживљај.
(Eez-lozh-bah mee yeh proo-zhee-lah fahn-tah-stee-chan doh-zhee-vlyahy.)

626. The concert was nothing short of fantastic.
Концерт је био заиста фантастичан.
(Kon-tsehrt yeh bee-oh zah-ee-stah fahn-tah-stee-chan.)

627. I'm still on cloud nine after the event.
Још увек сам на седмом небу након догађаја.
(Yosh oo-vehk sahm nah sehd-mohm neh-boo nah-kohn doh-gah-dzhai-ah.)

Travel Story: On a hike through Tara National Park, an adventurer described the scenery as, "Природа као слика," which means "Nature like a painting."

628. I was quite underwhelmed by the show.
Шоу ме је прилично разочарало.
(*Show me yeh pree-leech-noh rah-zoh-cha-rah-loh.*)

629. I expected more from the movie.
Очекивао/ла сам више од филма.
(*Oh-cheh-kee-vah-oh/lah sahm vee-sheh od feel-mah.*)

630. Unfortunately, the exhibition didn't impress me.
Нажалост, изложба ме није импресионирала.
(*Nah-zha-lost, eez-lozh-bah meh nee-ye eem-preh-see-oh-nee-rah-lah.*)

66
"Кад на врби роди грожђе."
"When grapes grow on a willow tree."
Something that is very unlikely to happen.
99

Mini Lesson:
Basic Grammar Principles in Serbian #2

Introduction:

Welcome back to our exploration of Serbian grammar. Building on the concepts covered in part 1, this lesson will delve into additional key aspects of Serbian grammar that are vital for developing a more comprehensive understanding of the language.

1. Word Order:

In Serbian, the basic sentence structure is Subject-Verb-Object (SVO), similar to English. However, due to its case system, Serbian enjoys a flexible word order, allowing for emphasis to be placed on different parts of the sentence.

- *Ја читам књигу. (I am reading a book.)*
- *Књигу читам ја. (The book is being read by me.)*

2. Reflexive Pronouns:

Serbian uses reflexive pronouns to indicate that the subject of the verb is also its object. These are often used in daily conversation.

- *Он се буди. (He wakes up [himself].)*
- *Ми се видимо. (We see each other.)*

3. The Imperative Mood:

Used to give commands or make requests, the imperative mood in Serbian changes according to the verb.

- *Реци ми! (Tell me!)*
- *Дођи овде! (Come here!)*

4. Compound Past Tense:

While Serbian has several past tenses, the compound past (perfekat) is commonly used in everyday conversation, formed with the auxiliary verb biti (to be) and the past participle of the main verb.

- *Ја сам прочитао књигу. (I have read the book.)*
- *Она је видела филм. (She has seen the movie.)*

5. The Conditional Mood:

The conditional mood is used to express wishes, hypotheses, or actions that are contingent on certain conditions. It's formed with the conditional of the auxiliary verb biti and the past participle.

- *Да сам знао, дошао бих. (If I had known, I would have come.)*

6. Adjective Agreement:

In Serbian, adjectives agree in gender, number, and case with the nouns they describe.

- *Велика кућа (big house - feminine)*
- *Велики ауто (big car - masculine)*

7. Possessive Pronouns:

Possessive pronouns in Serbian must agree in gender, number, and case with the noun they are describing.

- *Moja књига (My book - feminine)*
- *Moj ауто (My car - masculine)*

Conclusion:

Understanding these aspects of Serbian grammar will further enhance your ability to communicate effectively. As always, practice is essential, so immerse yourself in the language as much as possible. Srećno! (Good luck!)

HEALTHCARE & MEDICAL NEEDS

- EXPLAINING SYMPTOMS TO A DOCTOR -
- REQUESTING MEDICAL ASSISTANCE -
- DISCUSSING MEDICATIONS AND TREATMENT -

Explaining Symptoms

631.   I have a persistent headache.
Имам упорну главобољу.
(Ee-mam oo-por-noo glav-o-boh-lyoo.)

632.   My throat has been sore for a week.
Већ недељу дана имам бол у грлу.
(Vehch neh-delyoo dah-nah ee-mam bol oo grloo.)

633.   I've been experiencing stomach pain and nausea.
Имам болове у стомаку и мучнину.
(Ee-mam boh-loh-veh oo sto-mah-koo ee mooch-nee-noo.)

634.   I have a high fever and chills.
Имам високу температуру и дрхтавицу.
(Ee-mam vee-soh-koo tehm-peh-rah-too-roo ee drh-tah-vee-tsoo.)

635.   My back has been hurting for a few days.
Већ неколико дана ме боли леђа.
(Vehch neh-koh-lee-koh dah-nah meh boh-lee leh-jah.)

636.   I'm coughing up yellow mucus.
Кашљем жути шлегм.
(Kash-lyehm zhoo-tee shleh-gm.)

637.   I have a rash on my arm.
Имам осип на руци.
(Ee-mam oh-seep nah roo-tsee.)

> **Fun Fact:** Serbian swear words are known for their creativity and expressiveness.

638. I've been having trouble breathing.
Имам проблема са дисањем.
(*Ee-mam proh-bleh-mah sah dee-sah-nyehm.*)

639. I feel dizzy and lightheaded.
Осећам вртоглавицу и слабост.
(*Oh-seh-cham vrt-oh-glavee-tsoo ee slah-bost.*)

640. My joints are swollen and painful.
Зглобови су ми отечени и болни.
(*Zglo-boh-vee soo mee oh-teh-cheh-nee ee bol-nee.*)

641. I've had diarrhea for two days.
Имам пролив већ два дана.
(*Ee-mam proh-leev vehch dvah dah-nah.*)

642. My eyes are red and itchy.
Очи су ми црвене и сврбе.
(*Oh-chee soo mee tsrveh-neh ee svr-beh.*)

643. I've been vomiting since last night.
Повраћам од прошле ноћи.
(*Pov-rah-cham od proh-shleh noh-chee.*)

644. I have a painful, persistent toothache.
Имам болан и упоран зубобол.
(*Ee-mam boh-lahn ee oo-poh-rahn zoo-boh-bol.*)

645. I'm experiencing fatigue and weakness.
Осећам умор и слабост.
(*Oh-seh-cham oo-mor ee slah-bost.*)

646.   I've noticed blood in my urine.
Приметио/ла сам крв у урину.
(*Pree-me-tee-oh/lah sahm krv oo oo-ree-noo.*)

647.   My nose is congested, and I can't smell anything.
Нос ми је запушен и не могу да осетим мирисе.
(*Nos mee ye zah-poosh-en ee neh moh-goo dah oh-seh-teem mee-ree-seh.*)

648.   I have a cut that's not healing properly.
Имам рез који се не зараства како треба.
(*Ee-mahm rez koy-ee seh neh zah-ras-tvah kah-koh treh-bah.*)

649.   My ears have been hurting, and I can't hear well.
Уши ме боле и не чујем добро.
(*Oo-shee meh boh-leh ee neh choo-yehm doh-broh.*)

650.   I think I might have a urinary tract infection.
Мислим да имам инфекцију уринарног тракта.
(*Mees-leem dah ee-mahm een-fek-tsee-yoo oo-ree-nahr-nog trahk-tah.*)

651.   I've had trouble sleeping due to anxiety.
Имам проблема са спавањем због анксиозности.
(*Ee-mahm proh-bleh-mah sah spah-vah-nyehm zbog ahnk-see-ohz-nos-tee.*)

Requesting Medical Assistance

652.   I need to see a doctor urgently.
Хитно ми треба да видим лекара.
(*Heet-noh mee treh-bah dah vee-deem leh-kah-rah.*)

653. Can you call an ambulance, please?
Можете ли да позовете хитну помоћ, молим вас?
(*Moh-zheh-teh lee dah poh-zoh-veh-teh heet-noo poh-moch, moh-leem vahs?*)

> **Travel Story:** At a pottery workshop in Zlakusa village, a craftsman described his art as, "Традиција која живи," which translates to "A tradition that lives."

654. I require immediate medical attention.
Хитно ми је потребна медицинска помоћ.
(*Heet-noh mee ye poh-treb-nah meh-dee-tseen-skah poh-moch.*)

655. Is there an available appointment today?
Има ли слободан термин данас?
(*Ee-mah lee sloh-boh-dahn tehr-meen dah-nahs?*)

656. Please help me find a nearby clinic.
Молим вас, помозите ми да пронађем блиску клинику.
(*Moh-leem vahs, poh-moh-zee-teh mee dah proh-nah-dyehm blees-koo klee-nee-koo.*)

657. I think I'm having a medical emergency.
Мислим да имам хитну медицинску ситуацију.
(*Mees-leem dah ee-mahm heet-noo meh-dee-tseen-skoo see-too-ah-tsee-yoo.*)

658. Can you recommend a specialist?
Можете ли да препоручите специјалисту?
(*Moh-zheh-teh lee dah preh-poh-roo-chee-teh speh-tsee-yah-lees-too?*)

659. I'm in severe pain; can I see a doctor now?
Имам јаке болове; могу ли одмах да видим лекара?
(*Ee-mahm yah-keh boh-loh-veh; moh-goo lee od-mahk dah vee-deem leh-kah-rah?*)

660. Is there a 24-hour pharmacy in the area?
Да ли има 24-часовну апотеку у овом подручју?
(Dah lee ee-ma dvah-deset ee chetiri chah-sov-noo ah-po-teh-koo oo oh-vohm poh-droo-chyoo?)

661. I need a prescription refill.
Потребно ми је поновно издавање рецепта.
(Poh-treb-no mee ye poh-nohv-noh eez-dah-vah-nyeh reh-tsep-tah.)

662. Can you guide me to the nearest hospital?
Можете ли ме упутити до најближе болнице?
(Moh-zheh-teh lee meh oo-poo-tee-tee doh nai-blee-zheh bohl-nee-tseh?)

663. I've cut myself and need medical assistance.
Исекао/секла сам се и потребна ми је медицинска помоћ.
(Ee-seh-kah-oh/seh-klah sahm seh ee poh-treb-nah mee ye meh-dee-tseen-skah poh-moch.)

664. My child has a high fever; what should I do?
Моје дете има високу температуру; шта да радим?
(Moy-eh deh-teh ee-mah vee-soh-koo tehm-peh-rah-too-roo; shta dah rah-deem?)

665. Is there a walk-in clinic nearby?
Да ли има клиника за хитне случајеве у близини?
(Dah lee ee-mah klee-nee-kah zah heet-neh sloo-cha-ye-veh oo bleh-zee-nee?)

666. I need medical advice about my condition.
Потребан ми је медицински савет за моје стање.
(Poh-treh-bahn mee ye meh-dee-tseen-skee sah-veht zah moy-eh stah-nyeh.)

667. My medication has run out; I need a refill.
Лекови су ми потрошени; потребно ми је поновно издавање.
(*Leh-koh-vee soo mee poh-troh-sheh-nee; poh-treb-no mee ye poh-nohv-noh eez-dah-vah-nyeh.*)

668. Can you direct me to an eye doctor?
Можете ли ме упутити до офталмолога?
(*Moh-zheh-teh lee meh oo-poo-tee-tee doh of-tahl-moh-loh-gah?*)

669. I've been bitten by a dog; I'm concerned.
Ујео/ујела ме је пас; забринут/а сам.
(*Oo-yeh-oh/oo-yeh-lah meh ye pas; zah-bree-noot/ah sahm.*)

670. Is there a dentist available for an emergency?
Да ли је доступан стоматолог за хитне случајеве?
(*Dah lee ye doos-too-pahn stoh-mah-toh-loh-gah zah heet-neh sloo-cha-ye-veh?*)

671. I think I might have food poisoning.
Мислим да имам тровање храном.
(*Mees-leem dah ee-mam troh-vah-nyeh hrah-nohm.*)

672. Can you help me find a pediatrician for my child?
Можете ли ми помоћи да пронађем педијатра за моје дете?
(*Moh-zheh-teh lee mee poh-moh-tchee dah proh-nah-jehm peh-dee-yah-trah zah moy-eh deh-teh?*)

> **Idiomatic Expression:** "Од очију да те склоним." - Meaning: "I wish you were out of my sight." (Literal translation: "To move you out of my eyes.")

Discussing Medications and Treatments

673.   What is this medication for?
За шта је овај лек?
(Zah shta ye oh-vai lek?)

674.   How often should I take this pill?
Колико често треба да узимам ову пилулу?
*(Koh-lee-koh ches-toh treh-bah dah oo-zee-mahm oh-voo
pee-loo-loo?)*

675.   Are there any potential side effects?
Да ли има потенцијалних нежељених ефеката?
*(Dah lee ee-mah poh-ten-tsee-yahl-nee-h nezhe-lye-nee-h
eh-fek-ah-tah?)*

676.   Can I take this medicine with food?
Да ли могу да узмем овај лек са храном?
(Dah lee moh-goo dah ooz-mem oh-vai lek sah hrah-nom?)

677.   Should I avoid alcohol while on this medication?
Да ли треба да избегавам алкохол док узимам овај лек?
*(Dah lee treh-bah dah eez-beh-gah-vahm ahl-koh-hohl dok
oo-zee-mahm oh-vai lek?)*

678.   Is it safe to drive while taking this?
Да ли је безбедно вожња док узимам овај лек?
*(Dah lee ye behz-behd-noh vohzh-nyah dok oo-zee-mahm
oh-vai lek?)*

679.   Are there any dietary restrictions?
Да ли постоје дијетална ограничења?
(Dah lee poh-stoy-ye dee-ye-tahl-nah oh-grah-nee-cheh-nyah?)

680. Can you explain the dosage instructions?
Можете ли објаснити упутства за дозирање?
(*Moh-zheh-teh lee ob-yahs-nee-tee oo-poot-stvah zah doh-zee-rah-nyeh?*)

681. What should I do if I miss a dose?
Шта да радим ако пропустим дозу?
(*Shta dah rah-deem ah-koh proh-poo-steem doh-zoo?*)

682. How long do I need to continue this treatment?
Колико дуго треба да наставим овај третман?
(*Koh-lee-koh doo-goh treh-bah dah nah-stah-veem oh-vai treht-mahn?*)

683. Can I get a generic version of this medication?
Да ли могу добити генеричку верзију овог лека?
(*Dah lee moh-goo doh-bee-tee geh-neh-reech-koo vehr-zee-yoo oh-vohg leh-kah?*)

684. Is there a non-prescription alternative?
Да ли постоји алтернатива без рецепта?
(*Dah lee poh-stoy-ee ahl-tehr-nah-tee-vah behz reh-tsehp-tah?*)

685. How should I store this medication?
Како треба да чувам овај лек?
(*Kah-koh treh-bah dah choo-vahm oh-vai lek?*)

686. Can you show me how to use this inhaler?
Можете ли ми показати како да користим овај инхалатор?
(*Moh-zheh-teh lee mee poh-kah-zah-tee kah-koh dah koh-ree-steem oh-vai een-hah-lah-tor?*)

687. What's the expiry date of this medicine?
Који је рок трајања овог лека?
(Koyi ye rok trah-yan-ya ovog leka?)

> **Fun Fact:** Traditional Serbian music encompasses a variety of genres and styles.

688. Do I need to finish the entire course of antibiotics?
Да ли треба да завршим цео курс антибиотика?
(Da li treba da završim ceo kurs antibiotika?)

689. Can I cut these pills in half?
Могу ли да преполовим ове пилуле?
(Mogu li da prepolovim ove pilule?)

690. Is there an over-the-counter pain reliever you recommend?
Препоручујете ли неки безрецептни аналгетик?
(Preporučujete li neki bezreceptni analgetik?)

691. Can I take this medication while pregnant?
Могу ли да узимам овај лек током трудноће?
(Mogu li da uzimam ovaj lek tokom trudnoće?)

692. What should I do if I experience an allergic reaction?
Шта да радим ако доживим алергијску реакцију?
(Šta da radim ako doživim alergijsku reakciju?)

> **Fun Fact:** The Smederevo Fortress is one of Europe's largest medieval fortresses.

693.   Can you provide more information about this treatment plan?
Можете ли дати више информација о овом плану лечења?
(*Možete li dati više informacija o ovom planu lečenja?*)

"После кише дође сунце."
"After the rain comes the sun."
Good times follow bad times.

Word Search Puzzle: Healthcare

HOSPITAL
БОЛНИЦА
DOCTOR
ЛЕКАР
MEDICINE
ЛЕК
PRESCRIPTION
РЕЦЕПТ
APPOINTMENT
ТЕРМИН
SURGERY
ХИРУРГИЈА
VACCINE
ВАКЦИНА
PHARMACY
АПОТЕКА
ILLNESS
БОЛЕСТ
TREATMENT
ЛЕЧЕЊЕ
DIAGNOSIS
ДИЈАГНОЗА
RECOVERY
ОПОРАВАК
SYMPTOM
СИМПТОМ
IMMUNIZATION
ИМУНИЗАЦИЈА

```
K R A C Q D Б I T I Y R Б T A
V E M Z O T O K O G M S O E H
A D E C S A Л D X N U W Л Р И
X C T Р Е Ц Е П T R H R H M Ц
H O N J F T C E G S Z B И И K
R Y I A A U T E N O H N Ц H A
E Њ E Ч Е Л R S B I O Y A S B
G J Q L Q Y O N A I C T K Y C
B M W F T D F K T A R C R I A
I F Р A K Е Л P M E N E A P J
W S R O H F I R A V V D D V B
F G Y G N R A T X O Y I E A T
R U S M C H M L C E N B K З L
A N D S P E S E V C V P T O P
C M E B N T R I Z Q H M A H N
T R Q T V K O O S H D Q S Г R
P A L R M A P M F O R P O A H
A P P A П O T E K A N M E J H
R J Z P D B Y O S F C G S И D
E I И C O Y L H D K И H A Д P
T N L Ц E I Q A B J M U K I M
W C I L A H N M R T П V E N D
R T C C N З O T S W T M Л K K
R X I T I E И S M L O L O E T
F Z T S C D S H P E M F B L C
J G D Z N Y E S У I N J L V N
K E E E N B G M T M T T Q S B
T U O П O P A B A K И A Q N R
N O I T A Z I N U M M I L A D
A J И Г P У P И X T Z G I S M
```

158

Correct Answers:

FAMILY & RELATIONSHIPS

- TALKING ABOUT FAMILY MEMBERS & RELATIONSHIPS -
- DISCUSSING PERSONAL LIFE & EXPERIENCES -
- EXPRESSING EMOTIONS & SENTIMENTS -

Family Members and Relationships

694. He's my younger brother.
Он је мој млађи брат.
(On ye moy mladji brat.)

695. She's my cousin from my mother's side.
Она је моја рођака са мајчине стране.
(Ona ye moy-a rodjaka sa maj-chine strane.)

696. My grandparents have been married for 50 years.
Моји бака и деда су у браку 50 година.
(Moyi baka i deda su u braku pedeset godina.)

697. We're like sisters from another mister.
Ми смо као сестре, али из друге породице.
(Mi smo kao sestre, ali iz druge porodice.)

698. He's my husband's best friend.
Он је најбољи пријатељ мог супруга.
(On ye najbolji prijatelj mog supruga.)

699. She's my niece on my father's side.
Она је моја нећака са очеве стране.
(Ona ye moy-a nećaka sa očeve strane.)

700. They are my in-laws.
Они су моји свашта и ташта.
(Oni su moyi svašta i tašta.)

701. Our family is quite close-knit.
Наша породица је веома заједничка.
(*Nasha porodica ye veoma zajednička.*)

702. He's my adopted son.
Он је мој усвојени син.
(*On ye moy usvojeni sin.*)

703. She's my half-sister.
Она је моја полусестра.
(*Ona ye moy-a polusestra.*)

> **Travel Story:** While exploring the cobbled streets of Skadarlija, a visitor said, "Кораци кроз време," meaning "Steps through time," feeling the historic charm.

704. My parents are divorced.
Моји родитељи су разведени.
(*Moyi roditelji su razvedeni.*)

705. He's my fiancé.
Он је мој вереник.
(*On ye moy verenik.*)

706. She's my daughter-in-law.
Она је моја снаја.
(*Ona ye moy-a snaja.*)

> **Idiomatic Expression:** "Прогутати језик." -
> Meaning: "To be speechless."
> (Literal translation: "To swallow one's tongue.")

707. We're childhood friends.
Ми смо пријатељи из детињства.
(*Mi smo pri-ya-te-li iz de-tinj-stva.*)

708. My twin brother and I are very close.
Ја и мој брат близанац смо веома блиски.
(*Ya i moy brat bli-za-nats smo ve-oma bli-ski.*)

709. He's my godfather.
Он је мој кум.
(*On ye moy koom.*)

710. She's my stepsister.
Она је моја посестра.
(*O-na ye moy-a po-ses-tra.*)

711. My aunt is a world traveler.
Моја тетка је светски путник.
(*Moy-a tet-ka ye svet-ski put-nik.*)

712. We're distant relatives.
Ми смо далеки рођаци.
(*Mi smo da-le-ki rod-ja-tsi.*)

713. He's my brother-in-law.
Он је мој зет.
(*On ye moy zet.*)

714. She's my ex-girlfriend.
Она је моја бивша девојка.
(*O-na ye moy-a biv-sha de-voj-ka.*)

Personal Life and Experiences

715. I've traveled to over 20 countries.
Путовао сам у преко 20 земаља.
(Pu-to-vao sam u pre-ko dva-de-set ze-mlja.)

716. She's an avid hiker and backpacker.
Она је страствена планинарка и бекпекерка.
(O-na ye stras-tve-na pla-ni-nar-ka i bek-pe-ker-ka.)

717. I enjoy cooking and trying new recipes.
Волим кувати и пробавати нове рецепте.
(Vo-lim ku-va-ti i pro-ba-va-ti no-ve re-tsep-te.)

718. He's a professional photographer.
Он је професионални фотограф.
(On ye pro-fe-si-o-nal-ni fo-to-graf.)

719. I'm passionate about environmental conservation.
Страствен сам за заштиту животне средине.
(Stras-tven sam za zash-ti-tu zhi-vot-ne sre-di-ne.)

720. She's a proud dog owner.
Она је поносна власница пса.
(O-na ye po-nos-na vlas-ni-tsa psa.)

721. I love attending live music concerts.
Обожавам да идем на концерте уживо.
(O-bo-za-vam da i-dem na kon-tser-te u-zhi-vo.)

722. He's an entrepreneur running his own business.
Он је предузетник који води сопствени бизнис.
(*On ye pre-du-zet-nik koy-ee vo-dee sop-stve-nee beez-nees.*)

723. I've completed a marathon.
Завршио сам маратон.
(*Zav-rshee-oh sam ma-ra-ton.*)

724. She's a dedicated volunteer at a local shelter.
Она је предан волонтер у локалном прихватилишту.
(*O-na ye pre-dan vo-lon-ter oo lo-kal-nom pri-hva-tee-lisht-oo.*)

725. I'm a history buff.
Ја сам љубитељ историје.
(*Ya sam lyu-bee-te-ly is-to-ri-ye.*)

726. I'm a proud parent of three children.
Ја сам поносни родитељ троје деце.
(*Ya sam po-nos-nee ro-dee-tel tro-ye de-tse.*)

727. I've recently taken up painting.
Недавно сам почео да сликам.
(*Ne-dav-no sam po-che-o da slee-kam.*)

728. She's a film enthusiast.
Она је љубитељ филмова.
(*O-na ye lyu-bee-tel feel-mo-va.*)

729. I enjoy gardening in my free time.
Уживам у бављењу вртларством у слободно време.
(*Oo-zhee-vam oo bav-lye-nyoo vrt-lar-stvom oo slo-bo-dno vre-me.*)

730. He's an astronomy enthusiast.
Он је љубитељ астрономије.
(*On ye lyu-bee-tel as-tro-no-mi-ye.*)

731. I've skydived twice.
Скакао сам са падобраном два пута.
(*Ska-kao sam sa pa-do-bra-nom dva poo-ta.*)

732. She's a fitness trainer.
Она је фитнес тренер.
(*O-na ye fit-nes tre-ner.*)

733. I love collecting vintage records.
Волим да сакупљам винтиџ плоче.
(*Vo-leem da sa-koo-plyam vin-teej plo-che.*)

734. He's an experienced scuba diver.
Он је искусан ронилац.
(*On ye ees-koo-san ro-nee-lats.*)

735. He's a bookworm and a literature lover.
Он је књигомољац и љубитељ књижевности.
(*On ye knyee-go-mo-lya-ts ee lyu-bee-tel knyee-zhe-vnos-tee.*)

> **Fun Fact:** Serbian distinguishes between formal and informal speech.

Expressing Emotions and Sentiments

736. I feel overjoyed on my birthday.
Осећам се пресрећно на свој рођендан.
(*O-se-cham se pre-se-ch-no na svo-y rod-yen-dan.*)

737. She's going through a tough time right now.
Пролази кроз тежак период управо сада.
(Pro-la-zi kroz te-zhak pe-ri-od u-pra-vo sa-da.)

738. I'm thrilled about my upcoming vacation.
Узбуђен сам због предстојећег одмора.
(Uz-bu-jen sam zbog pred-sto-je-cheg od-mo-ra.)

739. He's heartbroken after the breakup.
Сломљен је након прекида.
(Slo-mljen ye na-kon pre-ki-da.)

740. I'm absolutely ecstatic about the news.
Потпуно сам одушевљен због вести.
(Pot-pu-no sam o-du-shev-ljen zbog ves-ti.)

741. She's feeling anxious before the big presentation.
Анксиозна је пред велику презентацију.
(An-ksi-oz-na ye pred ve-li-ku pre-zen-ta-tsi-ju.)

742. I'm proud of my team's achievements.
Поносан сам на достигнућа мог тима.
(Po-no-san sam na dos-tig-nu-cha mog ti-ma.)

743. He's devastated by the loss.
Уништен је због губитка.
(U-nish-ten ye zbog gu-bit-ka.)

744. I'm grateful for the support I received.
Захвалан сам на подршци коју сам добио.
(*Zah-va-lan sam na pod-rsh-ki ko-ju sam do-bi-o.*)

745. She's experiencing a mix of emotions.
Доживљава мешавину осећања.
(*Do-zhi-vlja-va me-sha-vi-nu o-se-cha-nja.*)

746. I'm content with where I am in life.
Задовољан сам са тим где сам у животу.
(*Za-do-vo-ljan sam sa tim gde sam u zhi-vo-tu.*)

747. He's overwhelmed by the workload.
Преоптерећен је радним обимом.
(*Pre-op-te-re-chen ye rad-nim o-bi-mom.*)

748. I'm in awe of the natural beauty here.
Одушевљен сам природном лепотом овде.
(*O-du-shev-ljen sam pri-rod-nom le-po-tom ov-de.*)

> **Language Learning Tip:** Learn Serbian Songs - Singing can improve pronunciation and intonation.

749. She's relieved the exams are finally over.
Олакшана је што су испити коначно завршени.
(*O-lak-sha-na ye shto su is-pi-ti ko-nach-no za-vrsh-e-ni.*)

750. I'm excited about the new job opportunity.
Узбуђен сам због нове могућпости за посао.
(*Uz-bu-jen sam zbog no-ve mo-gu-ch-no-sti za po-sao.*)

Travel Story: During a boat ride on the Danube, a local guide used the expression, "Река која спаја," meaning "The river that connects," highlighting the Danube's importance.

751.   I'm nostalgic about my childhood.
       Носталгичан сам за своје детињство.
       (Nos-tal-gee-chan sam za svo-ye deh-teenj-stvo.)

752.   She's confused about her future.
       Она је збуњена око своје будућности.
       (O-na ye zboo-nye-na o-ko svo-ye boo-dooch-nos-tee.)

753.   I'm touched by the kindness of strangers.
       Дирнут сам љубазношћу непознатих.
       (Deer-noot sam lyoo-baz-nosh-choo neh-poz-nah-tee-h.)

754.   He's envious of his friend's success.
       Завиди на успеху свог пријатеља.
       (Za-vee-dee na oos-pe-hoo svog pree-ya-te-lya.)

755.   I'm hopeful for a better tomorrow.
       Надам се бољем сутра.
       (Na-dam se bo-lyem soo-tra.)

> "Ум је мања боља."
> **"Mind is a better servant."**
> *It's better to rely on intellect than on physical strength.*

Interactive Challenge: Family & Relationships
(Link each English word with their corresponding meaning in Serbian)

1) Family	Браћа и сестре
2) Parents	Рођаци
3) Siblings	Пријатељство
4) Children	Супружник
5) Grandparents	Развод
6) Spouse	Родитељи
7) Marriage	Деца
8) Love	Бака и деда
9) Friendship	Љубав
10) Relatives	Породица
11) In-laws	Рођаци (први рођаци)
12) Divorce	Усвојење
13) Adoption	Нећака
14) Cousins	Брак
15) Niece	Свекрва и свекар / Ташта и таст

Correct Answers:

1. Family - Породица
2. Parents - Родитељи
3. Siblings - Браћа и сестре
4. Children - Деца
5. Grandparents - Бака и деда
6. Spouse - Супружник
7. Marriage - Брак
8. Love - Љубав
9. Friendship - Пријатељство
10. Relatives - Рођаци
11. In-laws - Свекрва и свекар / Ташта и таст
12. Divorce - Развод
13. Adoption - Усвојење
14. Cousins - Рођаци (први рођаци)
15. Niece - Нећака

TECHNOLOGY & COMMUNICATION

- USING TECHNOLOGY-RELATED PHRASES -
- INTERNET ACCESS AND COMMUNICATION TOOLS -
- TROUBLESHOOTING TECHNICAL ISSUES -

Using Technology

756.   I use my smartphone for various tasks.
Користим свој смартфон за разне задатке.
(Ko-ree-stim svo-y sma-rtfon za raz-ne za-dat-ke.)

757.   The computer is an essential tool in my work.
Компјутер је суштински алат у мом послу.
(Kom-pju-ter ye soosh-tin-skee a-lat u mom po-slu.)

758.   I'm learning how to code and develop software.
Учим како да програмирам и развијам софтвер.
(Oo-cheem ka-ko da pro-gra-mee-ram ee raz-vee-yam soft-ver.)

759.   My tablet helps me stay organized.
Таблет ми помаже да останем организован.
(Ta-blet mee po-ma-zhe da os-ta-nem or-ga-ni-zo-van.)

760.   I enjoy exploring new apps and software.
Волим да истражујем нове апликације и софтвер.
(Vo-leem da ees-trah-zhoo-yem no-ve ap-li-ka-tsi-ye ee soft-ver.)

> **Fun Fact:** In Serbian, many words have different meanings based on context.

761.   Smartwatches are becoming more popular.
Паметни сатови постају све популарнији.
(Pa-met-nee sa-to-vee pos-ta-yoo sve po-poo-lar-nee-yee.)

762. Virtual reality technology is fascinating.
Технологија виртуелне стварности је фасцинантна.
(*Teh-no-lo-gi-ya veer-too-el-ne stvar-nos-tee ye fas-tsi-nant-na.*)

763. Artificial intelligence is changing industries.
Вештачка интелигенција мења индустрије.
(*Vesh-tach-ka in-te-li-gen-tsi-ya men-ya in-doos-tree-ye.*)

764. I like to customize my gadgets.
Волим да прилагођавам моје уређаје.
(*Vo-leem da pree-la-go-dzhavam mo-ye oo-re-dzhai-ye.*)

765. E-books have replaced physical books for me.
Е-књиге су замениле папирне књиге за мене.
(*E-knjee-ge soo za-me-nee-le pa-peer-ne knjee-ge za me-ne.*)

766. Social media platforms connect people worldwide.
Социјалне мреже повезују људе широм света.
(*So-tsi-yal-ne mre-zhe po-ve-zoo-yoo lyoo-de shee-rom sve-ta.*)

767. I'm a fan of wearable technology.
Фан сам носиве технологије.
(*Fan sam no-see-ve teh-no-lo-gi-ye.*)

768. The latest gadgets always catch my eye.
Најновији гаџети увек привлаче моју пажњу.
(*Naj-no-vee-yee gad-zhe-tee oo-vek pree-vla-che mo-yoo pa-zhnyoo.*)

769. My digital camera captures high-quality photos.
Мој дигитални фотоапарат прави фотографије високог квалитета.
(*Moy di-gi-tal-nee fo-to-a-pa-rat pra-vi fo-to-gra-fi-ye vi-so-kog kva-li-te-ta.*)

770. Home automation simplifies daily tasks.
Аутоматизација дома поједностављује свакодневне задатке.
(*Au-to-ma-ti-za-tsi-ya do-ma po-yed-no-stav-lyoo-ye sva-ko-dnev-ne za-dat-ke.*)

771. I'm into 3D printing as a hobby.
Занима ме 3D штампа као хоби.
(*Za-nee-ma me 3D shtam-pa kao ho-bi.*)

772. Streaming services have revolutionized entertainment.
Стриминг услуге су револуционирале забаву.
(*Stre-ming oos-loo-ge soo re-vo-lu-tsi-o-nee-ra-le za-ba-vu.*)

773. The Internet of Things (IoT) is expanding.
Интернет ствари (IoT) се шири.
(*In-ter-net stva-ri (IoT) se shee-ri.*)

774. I'm into gaming, both console and PC.
Волим играње на конзоли и рачунару.
(*Vo-leem ee-gra-nye na kon-zo-li i ra-choo-na-ru.*)

775. Wireless headphones make life more convenient.
Бежичне слушалице чине живот удобнијим.
(*Bez-i-chne sloo-sha-lee-tse chee-ne zhi-vot oo-dob-nee-yim.*)

776. Cloud storage is essential for my work.
Облачно складиштење је важно за мој рад.
(*Ob-lach-no skla-deesh-te-nye ye vazh-no za moy rad.*)

> **Travel Story:** In a vibrant street in Belgrade during the Night of Museums, an attendee said, "Култура у ваздуху," translating to "Culture in the air."

Internet Access and Communication Tools

777. I rely on high-speed internet for work.
Ослањам се на брз интернет за посао.
(*Os-lan-yam se na brz in-ter-net za po-sao.*)

778. Video conferencing is crucial for remote meetings.
Видео конференције су кључне за даљинске састанке.
(*Vi-de-o kon-fe-ren-tsi-ye soo klyuch-ne za dal-jin-ske sa-stan-ke.*)

779. Social media helps me stay connected with friends.
Социјалне мреже ми помажу да останем повезан са пријатељима.
(*So-tsi-yal-ne mre-zhe mi po-ma-zhoo da os-ta-nem po-ve-zan sa pree-ya-te-lyee-ma.*)

780. Email is my primary mode of communication.
Имејл је мој основни начин комуникације.
(*Ee-meyl ye moy os-nov-nee na-chin ko-mu-ni-ka-tsi-ye.*)

781. I use messaging apps to chat with family.
      Користим апликације за ћаскање са породицом.
      (*Ko-ree-steem apli-ka-tsi-ye za tcha-ska-nye sa po-ro-di-tsom.*)

782. Voice and video calls keep me in touch with loved ones.
      Гласовни и видео позиви ме држе у контакту са вољенима.
      (*Glas-ov-nee i vi-de-o po-zi-vi me dr-zhe u kon-tak-tu sa vol-ye-ni-ma.*)

783. Online forums are a great source of information.
      Онлајн форуми су одличан извор информација.
      (*On-lajn fo-ru-mi su od-li-tchan iz-vor in-for-ma-tsi-ya.*)

784. I trust encrypted messaging services for privacy.
      Верујем у шифроване услуге за поруке због приватности.
      (*Ve-roo-yem u shi-fro-va-ne oos-loo-ge za po-ru-ke zbog pri-vat-nos-ti.*)

785. Webinars are a valuable resource for learning.
      Вебинари су вредан ресурс за учење.
      (*Ve-bi-na-ri su vre-dan re-surs za u-che-nye.*)

> **Idiomatic Expression:** "Руке ми се не дижу." -
> Meaning: "I don't have the heart to do it."
> (Literal translation: "My hands don't lift.")

786. VPNs enhance online security and privacy.
      ВПН-ови побољшавају онлајн сигурност и приватност.
      (*VPN-ovi po-bolj-sha-vayu on-lajn si-gur-nost i pri-vat-nost.*)

787. Cloud-based collaboration tools are essential for teamwork.
Алати за сарадњу базирани на облаку су неопходни за тимски рад.
(A-la-ti za sa-rad-nyu ba-zi-ra-ni na ob-la-ku su ne-op-hod-ni za tim-ski rad.)

788. I prefer using a wireless router at home.
Више волим да користим бежични рутер код куће.
(Vi-she vo-leem da ko-ree-steem be-zhi-chnee ru-ter kod koo-tche.)

789. Online banking simplifies financial transactions.
Онлајн банкарство поједностављује финансијске трансакције.
(On-lajn ban-kar-stvo po-yed-no-stav-lyoo-ye fi-nan-si-ys-ke tran-sak-tsi-ye.)

> **Fun Fact:** Serbian literature is rich in both modern and classical works.

790. VoIP services are cost-effective for international calls.
VoIP услуге су економичне за међународне позиве.
(VoIP oos-loo-ge su e-ko-no-mich-ne za me-dzoo-na-rod-ne po-zi-ve.)

791. I enjoy online shopping for convenience.
Волим онлајн куповину због удобности.
(Vo-leem on-lajn koo-po-vi-nu zbog oo-dob-nos-ti.)

792. Social networking sites connect people globally.
Социјалне мреже повезују људе широм света.
(So-tsi-yal-ne mre-zhe po-ve-zoo-yoo lyoo-de shee-rom sve-ta.)

793.   E-commerce platforms offer a wide variety of products.
Е-трговина платформе нуде широк асортиман производа.
(*E-tr-go-vi-na plat-for-me noo-de shi-rok a-sor-ti-man pro-i-zvo-da.*)

> **Idiomatic Expression:** "Седети између две столице." - Meaning: "To be undecided."
> (Literal translation: "To sit between two chairs.")

794.   Mobile banking apps make managing finances easy.
Мобилне банкарске апликације олакшавају управљање финансијама.
(*Mo-bil-ne ban-kar-ske apli-ka-tsi-ye o-lak-sha-va-yoo oo-prav-lya-nje fi-nan-si-ya-ma.*)

795.   I'm active on professional networking sites.
Активан сам на професионалним мрежама за повезивање.
(*Ak-ti-van sam na pro-fe-si-o-nal-nim mre-zha-ma za po-ve-zi-va-nje.*)

796.   Virtual private networks protect my online identity.
Виртуелне приватне мреже штите мој онлајн идентитет.
(*Vir-tu-el-ne pri-vat-ne mre-zhe sh-ti-te moj on-lajn i-den-ti-tet.*)

797.   Instant messaging apps are great for quick chats.
Апликације за тренутно четовање су одличне за брзе разговоре.
(*Apli-ka-tsi-ye za tren-oot-no che-to-va-nje soo od-lich-ne za brze raz-go-vo-re.*)

> **Cultural Insight:** The majority of Serbians are Orthodox Christians, and this faith plays a significant role in their cultural identity.

Troubleshooting Technical Issues

798. My computer is running slow; I need to fix it.
Мој компјутер ради споро; треба да га поправим.
(Moj kom-pju-ter ra-di spo-ro; tre-ba da ga po-pra-vim.)

799. I'm experiencing network connectivity problems.
Имам проблеме са повезивањем мреже.
(I-mam pro-ble-me sa po-ve-zi-va-njem mre-zhe.)

800. The printer isn't responding to my print commands.
Штампач не реагује на моје наредбе за штампање.
(Shtam-pach ne re-a-goo-ye na mo-ye na-red-be za shtam-pa-nje.)

> **Fun Fact:** Serbian has a wealth of synonyms, adding to its expressiveness.

801. My smartphone keeps freezing; it's frustrating.
Мој смартфон стално замрзава; веома је фрустрирајуће.
(Moj smart-fon stal-no zam-rza-va; ve-o-ma ye frus-tri-ra-yoo-tche.)

802. The Wi-Fi signal in my house is weak.
Wi-Fi сигнал у мојој кући је слаб.
(Vee-Fee sig-nal oo mo-joj koo-tchi ye slab.)

803. I can't access certain websites; it's a concern.
Не могу да приступим одређеним вебсајтовима; то је забрињавајуће.
(Ne mo-goo da pris-too-pim o-dre-dye-nim veb-saj-to-vi-ma; to ye za brin ja va yoo-tche.)

804.   My laptop battery drains quickly; I need a solution.
Батерија мог лаптопа се брзо пражња; потребно ми је решење.
(*Ba-te-ri-ja mog lap-to-pa se brzo pra-zh-nja; po-treb-no mi ye re-she-nje.*)

805.   There's a software update available for my device.
Постоји доступно ажурирање софтвера за мој уређај.
(*Po-sto-ji do-stup-no a-zhu-ri-ra-nje soft-ve-ra za moj u-re-djaj.*)

806.   My email account got locked; I need to recover it.
Мој имејл налог је закључан; треба да га опоравим.
(*Moj i-mejl na-log ye zak-lju-chan; tre-ba da ga o-po-ra-vim.*)

> **Fun Fact:** Pronunciation and vocabulary in Serbian can vary significantly across regions.

807.   The screen on my tablet is cracked; I'm upset.
Екран мог таблета је пукнут; узнемирен сам.
(*Ek-ran mog ta-ble-ta ye puk-nut; uz-ne-mi-ren sam.*)

808.   My webcam isn't working during video calls.
Моја веб камера не ради током видео позива.
(*Mo-ja veb ka-me-ra ne ra-di to-kom vi-de-o po-zi-va.*)

809.   My phone's storage is almost full; I need to clear it.
Меморија мог телефона је скоро пуна; треба да је очистим.
(*Me-mo-ri-ja mog te-le-fo-na ye sko-ro pu-na; tre-ba da ye o-chi-stim.*)

810. I accidentally deleted important files; I need help.
Случајно сам избрисао важне фајлове; потребна ми је помоћ.
(*Slu-cha-jno sam iz-bri-sao vazh-ne faj-lo-ve; po-treb-na mi ye po-moch.*)

Fun Fact: Serbian retains some archaic Slavic words.

811. My smart home devices are not responding.
Моји паметни кућни уређаји не одговарају.
(*Mo-ji pa-met-ni kuch-ni u-re-djai ne od-go-va-ra-ju.*)

812. The GPS on my navigation app is inaccurate.
GPS на мојој навигационој апликацији је нетачан.
(*Je-Pe-Es na mo-joj na-vi-ga-tsi-o-noj apli-ka-tsi-ji ye ne-ta-chan.*)

813. My antivirus software detected a threat; I'm worried.
Мој антивирусни софтвер је открио претњу; забринут сам.
(*Moj an-ti-vi-rus-ni soft-ver ye ot-krio pre-tnju; za-bri-nut sam.*)

814. The touchscreen on my device is unresponsive.
Екран осетљив на додир мог уређаја не реагује.
(*Ek-ran o-set-ljiv na do-dir mog u-re-djaja ne re-a-gu-je.*)

815. My gaming console is displaying error messages.
Моја играчка конзола приказује поруке о грешци.
(*Mo-ja i-grach-ka kon-zo-la pri-ka-zu-je po-ru-ke o gre-shci.*)

Fun Fact: The Serbian Language Day is celebrated annually on February 21st.

816. I'm locked out of my social media account.
Избачен сам из мог социјалног медијског налога.
(*Iz-ba-chen sam iz mog so-tsi-jal-nog me-di-j-skog na-lo-ga.*)

817. The sound on my computer is distorted.
Звук на мом рачунару је искривљен.
(*Zvuk na mom ra-chu-na-ru ye is-kri-vljen.*)

818. My email attachments won't open; it's frustrating.
Прилози у мојем имејлу се не отварају; то је фрустрирајуће.
(*Pri-lo-zi u mo-jem i-mey-lu se ne ot-va-ra-ju; to ye frus-tri-ra-ju-che.*)

> "Ко рано рани, две среће граби."
> **"Who rises early, catches two fortunes."**
> *Starting early leads to more opportunities.*

Cross Word Puzzle: Technology & Communication

(Provide the English translation for the following Serbian words)

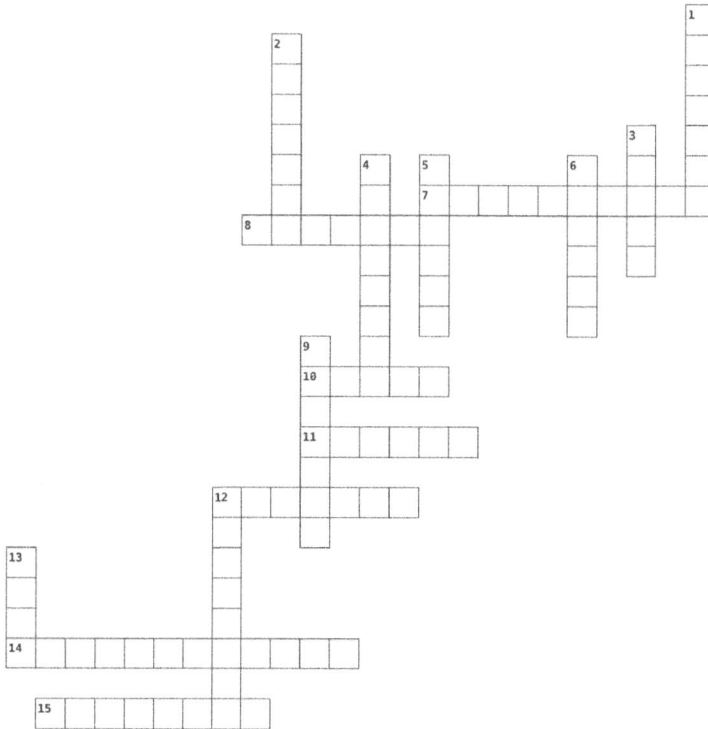

Down

1. - БАТЕРИЈА
2. - ПРЕТРАЖИВАЧ
3. - ОБЛАК
4. - ИНТЕРНЕТ
5. - ЕКРАН
6. - РУТЕР
9. - МРЕЖА
12. - КОМПЈУТЕР
13. - ПОДАЦИ

Across

7. - КРИПТОЛОГИЈА
8. - ШТАМПАЧ
10. - УЛАЗ
11. - ВЕБ КАМЕРА
12. - ПУЊАЧ
14. - АПЛИКАЦИЈЕ
15. - ТАСТАТУРА

185

Correct Answers:

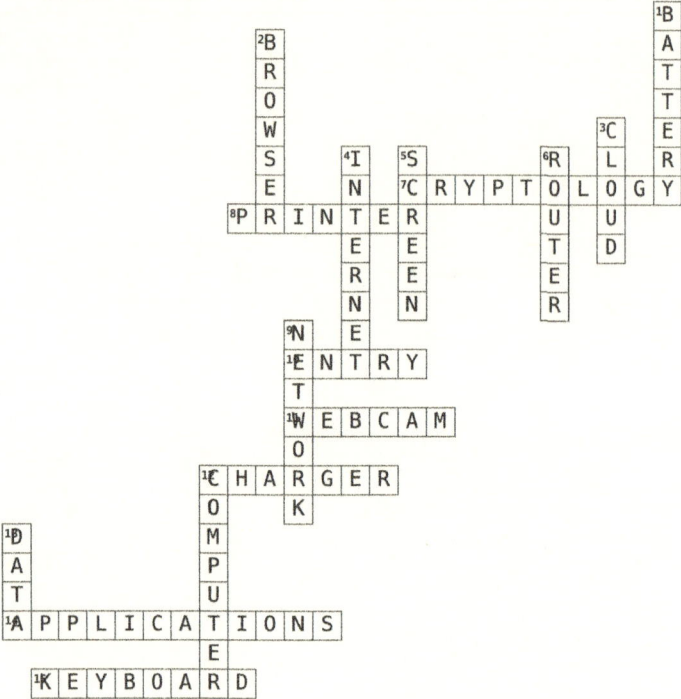

Across:
- 7. CRYPTOLOGY
- 8. PRINTER
- 10. ENTRY
- 11. WEBCAM
- 12. CHARGER
- 14. APPLICATIONS
- 15. KEYBOARD

Down:
- 1. BATTERY
- 2. BROWSE
- 3. CLOUD
- 4. INTERNET
- 5. SCREEN
- 6. ROUTER
- 9. NETWORK
- 13. COMPUTER
- 14. DATA

SPORTS & RECREATION

- DISCUSSING SPORTS, GAMES, & OUTDOOR ACTIVITIES -
- PARTICIPATING IN RECREATIONAL ACTIVITIES -
- EXPRESSING ENTHUSUASM OR FRUSTRATION -

Sports, Games, & Outdoor Activities

819.   I love playing soccer with my friends.
        Волим да играм фудбал са пријатељима.
        (*Vo-lim da ee-gram fud-bal sa pree-ya-te-lyi-ma.*)

820.   Basketball is a fast-paced and exciting sport.
        Кошарка је брз и узбудљив спорт.
        (*Ko-shar-ka ye brz ee uz-bud-ljiv sport.*)

821.   Let's go for a hike in the mountains this weekend.
        Хајде да идемо на планинарење овог викенда.
        (*Haj-de da ee-de-mo na pla-nee-na-re-nye o-vog vee-ken-da.*)

822.   Playing chess helps improve my strategic thinking.
        Играње шаха побољшава моје стратешко размишљање.
        (*Ee-gra-nye sha-ha po-bol-ja-va mo-ye stra-te-shko
        raz-mish-lya-nye.*)

823.   I'm a fan of tennis; it requires a lot of skill.
        Фан сам тениса; захтева пуно вештина.
        (*Fan sam te-nee-sa; zah-te-va poo-no ves-tee-na.*)

824.   Are you up for a game of volleyball at the beach?
        Да ли сте за игру одбојке на плажи?
        (*Da lee ste za ee-groo od-boj-ke na pla-zhi?*)

825.   Let's organize a game of ultimate frisbee.
        Да организујемо игру ултимат фризбија.
        (*Da or-ga-nee-zu-ye-mo ee-groo ul-tee-mat friz-bee-ya.*)

826. Baseball games are a great way to spend the afternoon.
Бејзбол утакмице су одличан начин да проведете поподне.
(*Beyz-bol oo-tak-mee-tse soo od-lee-chan na-cheen da pro-ve-de-te po-po-dne.*)

827. Camping in the wilderness is so peaceful.
Камповање у дивљини је тако мирано.
(*Kam-po-va-nye oo deev-lyee-nee ye ta-ko mee-ra-no.*)

828. I enjoy swimming in the local pool.
Уживам да пливам у локалном базену.
(*Oo-zhee-vam da plee-vam oo lo-kal-nom ba-ze-noo.*)

829. I'm learning to play the guitar in my free time.
Учим да свирам гитару у свом слободном времену.
(*Oo-cheem da svee-ram gee-ta-roo oo svom slo-bo-dnom vre-me-noo.*)

830. Skiing in the winter is an exhilarating experience.
Скијање зими је узбудљиво искуство.
(*Skee-ya-nye zee-mee ye ooz-boo-dlji-vo ees-koo-stvo.*)

831. Going fishing by the lake is so relaxing.
Риболов поред језера је тако опуштајући.
(*Ree-bo-lov po-red ye-ze-ra ye ta-ko o-pooshta-yoo-chee.*)

832. We should have a board game night with friends.
Требало би да имамо вече друштвених игара са пријатељима.
(*Tre-ba-lo bee da ee-ma-mo ve-che droosh-tve-nee-h ee-ga-ra sa pree-ya-te-lyi-ma.*)

> **Travel Story:** At a traditional Serbian wedding, a guest commented on the joyful atmosphere with, "Свадба за памћење," meaning "A wedding to remember."

833. Martial arts training keeps me fit and disciplined.
Тренинг борилачких вештина ме држи у форми и дисциплинован.
(*Tre-neeng bo-ree-lach-kih vesh-tee-na me dr-zhee oo for-mee ee dees-tsee-plee-no-van.*)

834. I'm a member of a local running club.
Члан сам локалног тркачког клуба.
(*Chlan sam lo-kal-nog trka-chkog kloo-ba.*)

835. Playing golf is a great way to unwind.
Играње голфа је одличан начин за опуштање.
(*Ee-gra-nye gol-fa ye od-lee-chan na-cheen za o-poosht-a-nye.*)

> **Idiomatic Expression:** "Ставити прст на чело." -
> Meaning: "To think hard about something."
> (Literal translation: "To put a finger on the forehead.")

836. Yoga classes help me stay flexible and calm.
Јога часови ми помажу да останем флексибилан и смирен.
(*Yo-ga cha-so-vi mi po-ma-zhu da o-sta-nem flek-si-bi-lan i smi-ren.*)

837. I can't wait to go snowboarding this season.
Једва чекам да одем на сноубординг ове сезоне.
(*Yed-va che-kam da o-dem na sno-u-bor-ding o-ve se-zo-ne.*)

838. Going kayaking down the river is an adventure.
Кајакање низ реку је авантура.
(*Ka-ya-ka-nye niz re-ku ye a-van-too-ra.*)

839. Let's organize a picnic in the park.
Организујмо пикник у парку.
(*Or-ga-nee-zu-y-mo pik-nik oo par-koo.*)

Participating in Recreational Activities

840.   I enjoy painting landscapes as a hobby.
       Уживам у сликању пејзажа као хобију.
       (Oo-zhi-vam oo sli-ka-nyu pei-za-zha ka-o ho-bi-yoo.)

841.   Gardening is a therapeutic way to spend my weekends.
       Вртларење је терапијски начин да проводим викенде.
       (Vrt-la-re-nye ye te-ra-pi-y-ski na-chin da pro-vo-dim vi-ken-de.)

842.   Playing the piano is my favorite pastime.
       Свирање клавира је моја омиљена забава.
       (Svi-ra-nye kla-vi-ra ye mo-ya o-mil-ye-na za-ba-va.)

843.   Reading books helps me escape into different worlds.
       Читање књига ми помаже да побегнем у различите светове.
       (Chi-ta-nye knji-ga mi po-ma-zhe da po-be-gnem oo raz-li-chi-te sve-to-ve.)

844.   I'm a regular at the local dance classes.
       Редовно похађам локалне часове плеса.
       (Re-dov-no po-ha-dyam lo-kal-ne cha-so-ve ple-sa.)

845.   Woodworking is a skill I've been honing.
       Обрада дрвета је вештина коју усавршавам.
       (O-bra-da drv-e-ta ye vesh-ti-na ko-yu oo-sa-vrsha-vam.)

> **Idiomatic Expression:** "Чист као суза." -
> Meaning: "Completely innocent."
> (Literal translation: "Clean as a tear.")

846. I find solace in birdwatching at the nature reserve.
Налазим утеху у посматрању птица у природном резервату.
(*Na-la-zim oo-te-hu u pos-ma-tra-nju pti-tsa u pri-rod-nom re-zer-va-tu.*)

847. Meditation and mindfulness keep me centered.
Медитација и свесност ме држе фокусираног.
(*Me-di-ta-tsi-ja i sves-nost me drzhe fo-ku-si-ra-nog.*)

848. I've taken up photography to capture moments.
Почео сам да се бавим фотографијом да бих захватио тренутке.
(*Po-cheo sam da se ba-vim fo-to-gra-fi-jom da bih zah-va-tio tre-nut-ke.*)

849. Going to the gym is part of my daily routine.
Идене у теретану је део моје свакодневне рутине.
(*I-de-ne u te-re-ta-nu je de-o mo-je sva-ko-dnev-ne ru-ti-ne.*)

850. Cooking new recipes is a creative outlet for me.
Кување нових рецепата је мој креативни израз.
(*Ku-va-nje no-vih re-tse-pa-ta je moj kre-a-tiv-ni iz-raz.*)

851. Building model airplanes is a fascinating hobby.
Састављање модела авиона је фасцинантан хоби.
(*Sas-tav-lja-nje mo-de-la a-vi-o-na je fas-tsi-nan-tan ho-bi.*)

852. I love attending art exhibitions and galleries.
Волим да похађам изложбе уметности и галерије.
(*Vo-lim da po-ha-dzam iz-lozh-be oo-me-tno-sti i ga-le-ri-je.*)

853. Collecting rare stamps has been a lifelong passion.
Сакупљање ретких поштанских марака је моја животна страст.
(*Sa-kup-lja-nje ret-kih posh-tan-skih ma-ra-ka je mo-ja zhi-vot-na strast.*)

854. I'm part of a community theater group.
Члан сам аматерског позоришта у заједници.
(*Chlan sam a-ma-ter-sko-g po-zo-rish-ta u za-je-dni-tsi.*)

855. Birdwatching helps me connect with nature.
Посматрање птица ми помаже да се повежем са природом.
(*Pos-ma-tra-nje pti-tsa mi po-ma-zhe da se po-ve-zhem sa pri-ro-dom.*)

856. I'm an avid cyclist and explore new trails.
Страствени бициклиста сам и истражујем нове стазе.
(*Strast-ve-ni bi-tsi-kli-sta sam i is-tra-zhu-jem no-ve sta-ze.*)

857. Pottery classes allow me to express myself.
Часови керамике ми омогућавају да се изразим.
(*Cha-so-vi ke-ra-mi-ke mi o-mo-gu-cha-vaju da se iz-ra-zim.*)

858. Playing board games with family is a tradition.
Играње друштвених игара са породицом је традиција.
(*Ig-ra-nje drus-tve-nih i-ga-ra sa po-ro-di-tsom je tra-di-tsi-ja.*)

859. I'm practicing mindfulness through meditation.
Вежбам свесност кроз медитацију.
(*Vezh-bam sves-nost kroz me-di-ta-tsi-ju.*)

860. I enjoy long walks in the park with my dog.
Волим да шетам у парку са мојим псом.
(*Vo-lim da she-tam u par-ku sa mo-jim psom.*)

> **Travel Story:** In the historic town of Smederevo, a local described the fortress as, "Тврђава прича," translating to "The fortress tells a story."

Expressing Enthusiasm or Frustration

861. I'm thrilled we won the championship!
Одушевљен сам што смо освојили првенство!
(*O-doo-shev-ljen sam shto smo os-vo-ji-li prven-stvo!*)

862. Scoring that goal felt amazing.
Постизање тог гола је било невероватно.
(*Po-sti-za-nje tog go-la je bi-lo ne-ve-ro-vat-no.*)

863. It's so frustrating when we lose a game.
Веома је фрустрирајуће када изгубимо утакмицу.
(*Ve-o-ma je frus-ti-ra-ju-će ka-da iz-gu-bi-mo u-tak-mi-cu.*)

864. I can't wait to play again next week.
Једва чекам да поново играм следеће недеље.
(*Jed-va che-kam da po-no-vo ig-ram sle-de-će ne-de-lje.*)

> **Fun Fact:** Serbian allows for creative and flexible word formation.

865. Our team's performance was outstanding.
Извођење нашег тима је било изузетно.
(*Iz-vo-de-nje na-sheg ti-ma je bi-lo i-zu-ze-tno.*)

866. We need to practice more; we keep losing.
Треба више да тренирамо; стално губимо.
(*Tre-ba vi-she da tre-ni-ra-mo; stal-no gu-bi-mo.*)

867. I'm over the moon about our victory!
Пресрећан сам због наше победе!
(*Pre-sre-ćan sam zbo-g na-she po-be-de!*)

> **Language Learning Tip:** Use Serbian Subtitles - While watching English movies, use Serbian subtitles.

868. I'm an avid cyclist and explore new trails.
Страствени бициклиста сам и истражујем нове стазе.
(*Strast-ve-ni bi-tsi-klis-ta sam i is-tra-žu-jem no-ve sta-ze.*)

869. The referee's decision was unfair.
Одлука судије је била неспроведна.
(*Od-lu-ka su-di-je je bi-la nes-pra-ved-na.*)

870. We've been on a winning streak lately.
У последње време смо у низу победа.
(*U po-sled-nje vre-me smo u ni-zu po-be-da.*)

871. I'm disappointed in our team's performance.
Разочаран сам због извођења нашег тима.
(*Ra-zo-cha-ran sam zbo-g iz-vo-de-nja na-sheg ti-ma.*)

872.   The adrenaline rush during the race was incredible.
Адреналински удар током трке био је невероватан.
(Ad-re-na-lin-ski u-dar to-kom tr-ke bi-o je ne-ve-ro-va-tan.)

873.   We need to step up our game to compete.
Морамо да подигнемо нашу игру за такмичење.
(Mo-ra-mo da po-dig-ne-mo na-šu i-gru za tak-mi-če-nje.)

874.   Winning the tournament was a dream come true.
Победа на турниру је била остварење сна.
(Po-be-da na tur-ni-ru je bi-la os-tva-re-nje sna.)

875.   I was so close to scoring a goal.
Био сам тако близу да постигнем гол.
(Bi-o sam ta-ko bli-zu da po-stig-nem gol.)

876.   We should celebrate our recent win.
Требало би да прославимо нашу скорашњу победу.
(Tre-ba-lo bi da pro-sla-vi-mo na-šu sko-ra-šnju po-be-du.)

877.   Losing by a narrow margin is frustrating.
Изгубити са малом разликом је фрустрирајуће.
(Iz-gu-bi-ti sa ma-lom raz-li-kom je frus-ti-ra-ju-će.)

878.   Let's train harder to improve our skills.
Хајде да се више потрудимо да побољшамо наше вештине.
*(Haj-de da se vi-še po-tru-di-mo da po-bo-ljša-mo
na-še veš-ti-ne.)*

879. The match was intense from start to finish.
Утакмица је била интензивна од почетка до краја.
(*U-tak-mi-ca je bi-la in-ten-zi-vna od po-čet-ka do kra-ja.*)

880. I'm proud of our team's sportsmanship.
Поносан сам на спортско понашање нашег тима.
(*Po-no-san sam na spor-tsko po-na-ša-nje na-šeg ti-ma.*)

881. We've faced tough competition this season.
Ове сезоне смо се суочили са тешком конкуренцијом.
(*O-ve se-zo-ne smo se su-o-či-li sa teš-kom kon-ku-ren-ci-jom.*)

882. I'm determined to give it my all in the next game.
Одлучан сам да дам све од себе у следећој игри.
(*Od-lu-čan sam da dam sve od se-be u sle-de-ćoj ig-ri.*)

"Странац види боље него домаћин."
"A stranger sees better than the host."
An outsider often has a clearer perspective.

Mini Lesson:
Basic Grammar Principles in Serbian #3

Introduction:

In this third installment of our Serbian grammar series, we continue our journey into the more intricate aspects of the Serbian language. This lesson will explore advanced grammar concepts that are essential for a comprehensive understanding of Serbian, allowing for more sophisticated and nuanced communication.

1. Clitic Pronouns:

Serbian uses clitic pronouns which are unstressed and attached to other words in a sentence. They usually precede the verb.

- *Видим те. (I see you.)*
- *Дај ми то. (Give it to me.)*

2. Verb Aspect:

Serbian verbs have two aspects: imperfective (used for ongoing, habitual, or repeated actions) and perfective (used for completed actions). Understanding aspects is key to mastering Serbian verbs.

- *Читам књигу (imperfective - I am reading/I read a book [ongoing action])*
- *Прочитао/Прочитала сам књигу (perfective - I have read the book [completed action])*

3. Diminutives and Augmentatives:

Serbian uses diminutives and augmentatives to express smaller or larger forms or to convey endearment or disdain.

- *Кућа (house) - Кућица (small house, cottage)*
- *Пас (dog) - Псашче (puppy)*

4. Future Tense:

The future tense in Serbian is formed with the auxiliary verb "hteti" (to want) and the infinitive form of the main verb.

- *Хоћу да идем. (I will go.)*

5. Passive Voice:

Like English, Serbian can express the passive voice, though it's less common. It is usually formed with the verb "biti" (to be) and a passive participle.

- *Књига је прочитана. (The book has been read.)*

6. Reported Speech:

In reported speech, the tense of the verb changes similarly to English.

- *Он каже да иде. (He says he is going.)*
- *Она је рекла да је ишла. (She said she went.)*

7. Instrumental Case:

The instrumental case in Serbian, used after certain prepositions or to indicate the means by which something is done, often requires attention due to its distinct endings.

- *Пишем оловком. (I write with a pencil.)*

8. Subjunctive Mood:

Although not as prevalent as in some languages, the subjunctive mood in Serbian expresses doubt, wish, or hypothetical scenarios, often using "da" followed by the verb.

- *Било би добро да дођеш. (It would be good if you came.)*

Conclusion:

Mastering these advanced elements of Serbian grammar will enable you to form more complex sentences and understand nuanced expressions. As with any language, continued practice and exposure are essential for fluency. Srećno! (Good luck!)

TRANSPORT & DIRECTIONS

- ASKING FOR AND GIVING DIRECTIONS -
- USING TRANSPORTATION-RELATED PHRASES -

Asking for and Giving Directions

883.   Can you tell me how to get to the nearest subway station?
Можете ли ми рећи како да стигнем до најближе метро станице?
(Mo-zhe-te li mi re-ći ka-ko da stig-nem do naj-bli-že me-tro sta-ni-tse?)

884.   Excuse me, where's the bus stop for Route 25?
Извините, где је аутобуско стајалиште за линију број 25?
(Iz-vi-ni-te, gde ye au-to-bus-ko sta-ja-liš-te za li-ni-yu broj 25?)

885.   Could you give me directions to the city center?
Можете ли ми дати упутства за центар града?
(Mo-zhe-te li mi da-ti u-put-stva za cen-tar gra-da?)

886.   I'm looking for a good place to eat around here. Any recommendations?
Тражим добро место за јело овде у близини. Имате ли препоруке?
(Tra-žim do-bro me-sto za je-lo ov-de u bli-zi-ni. I-ma-te li pre-po-ru-ke?)

887.   Which way is the nearest pharmacy?
Који пут води до најближе апотеке?
(Ko-ji put vo-di do naj-bli-že a-po-te-ke?)

888.   How do I get to the airport from here?
Како да стигнем до аеродрома одавде?
(Ka-ko da stig-nem do a-e-ro-dro-ma o-dav-de?)

889. Can you point me to the nearest ATM?
Можете ли ми показати где је најближи банкомат?
(*Mo-zhe-te li mi po-ka-za-ti gde ye naj-bli-ži ban-ko-mat?*)

890. I'm lost. Can you help me find my way back to the hotel?
Изгубио/ла сам се. Можете ли ми помоћи да се вратим у хотел?
(*Iz-gu-bi-o/la sam se. Mo-zhe-te li mi po-mo-ći da se vra-tim u ho-tel?*)

891. Where's the closest gas station?
Где је најближа бензинска станица?
(*Gde ye naj-bli-ža ben-zin-ska sta-ni-tsa?*)

892. Is there a map of the city available?
Да ли постоји мапа града?
(*Da li po-sto-ji ma-pa gra-da?*)

893. How far is it to the train station from here?
Колико је далеко железничка станица одавде?
(*Ko-li-ko ye da-le-ko že-lez-nič-ka sta-ni-tsa o-dav-de?*)

894. Which exit should I take to reach the shopping mall?
Који излаз треба да узмем да бих стигао/ла до тржног центра?
(*Ko-ji iz-laz tre-ba da uz-mem da bih sti-ga-o/la do trž-nog cen-tra?*)

895. Where can I find a taxi stand around here?
Где могу да нађем такси стајалиште у овој области?
(*Gde mo-gu da na-đem tak-si sta-ja-liš-te u o-voj ob-la-sti?*)

896. Can you direct me to the main tourist attractions?
Можете ли ми указати пут до главних туристичких атракција?
(*Mo-zhe-te li mi u-ka-za-ti put do glav-nih tu-ris-ti-chkih a-trak-tsi-ja?*)

> **Fun Fact:** The Miroslav's Gospel is one of the oldest surviving documents written in Serbian.

897. I need to go to the hospital. Can you provide directions?
Треба ми да одем у болницу. Можете ли ми дати упутства?
(*Tre-ba mi da o-dem u bol-ni-tsu. Mo-zhe-te li mi da-ti u-put-stva?*)

898. Is there a park nearby where I can go for a walk?
Има ли у близини парк у који могу да прошетам?
(*I-ma li u bli-zi-ni park u ko-ji mo-gu da pro-she-tam?*)

899. Which street should I take to reach the museum?
Којом улицом треба да идем да бих стигао до музеја?
(*Ko-jom u-li-tsom tre-ba da id-em da bih sti-gao do mu-ze-ja?*)

900. How do I get to the concert venue?
Како да стигнем до места одржавања концерта?
(*Ka-ko da stig-nem do me-sta od-rzha-va-nja kon-tser-ta?*)

901. Can you guide me to the nearest public restroom?
Можете ли ми показати пут до најближе јавне тоалете?
(*Mo-zhe-te li mi po-ka-za-ti put do naj-bli-že jav-ne to-a-le-te?*)

902. Where's the best place to catch a cab in this area?

Где је најбоље место за ухватити такси у овој области?

(*Gde ye naj-bo-lje me-sto za uh-va-ti-ti tak-si u o-voj ob-las-ti?*)

Buying Tickets

903. I'd like to buy a one-way ticket to downtown, please.

Желим да купим једносмерну карту за центар, молим.

(*Zhe-lim da ku-pim jed-no-smer-nu kar-tu za cen-tar, mo-lim.*)

904. How much is a round-trip ticket to the airport?

Колико кошта повратна карта до аеродрома?

(*Ko-li-ko kosh-ta po-vrat-na kar-ta do ae-ro-dro-ma?*)

905. Do you accept credit cards for ticket purchases?

Да ли прихватате кредитне картице за куповину карата?

(*Da li pri-hva-ta-te kre-dit-ne kar-ti-tse za ku-po-vi-nu ka-ra-ta?*)

906. Can I get a student discount on this train ticket?

Да ли могу да добијем студентски попуст на ову возну карту?

(*Da li mo-gu da do-bi-jem stu-den-tski po-pust na o-vu vo-znu kar-tu?*)

907. Is there a family pass available for the bus?

Да ли постоји породична пропусница за аутобус?

(*Da li po-sto-ji po-ro-di-ch-na pro-pus-ni-tsa za au-to-bus?*)

> **Fun Fact:** Serbian has influenced neighboring Slavic languages.

908. What's the fare for a child on the subway?
Колика је цена карте за дете у метроу?
(*Ko-li-ka ye tse-na kar-te za de-te u me-tro-u?*)

909. Are there any senior citizen discounts for tram tickets?
Да ли постоје попусти за старије особе за трамвајске карте?
(*Da li po-sto-je po-pu-sti za sta-ri-je o-so-be za tram-vaj-ske kar-te?*)

910. Do I need to make a reservation for the express train?
Да ли треба да направим резервацију за експресни воз?
(*Da li tre-ba da na-pra-vim re-zer-va-tsi-ju za eks-pre-sni voz?*)

911. Can I upgrade to first class on this flight?
Да ли могу да пређем у прву класу на овом лету?
(*Da li mo-gu da pre-jem u pr-vu kla-su na o-vom le-tu?*)

912. Are there any extra fees for luggage on this bus?
Да ли има додатних накнада за пртљаг у овом аутобусу?
(*Da li i-ma do-dat-nih nak-na-da za prtl-jag u o-vom au-to-bu-su?*)

913. I'd like to book a sleeper car for the overnight train.
Желим да резервишем спаваћи вагон за ноћни воз.
(*Zhe-lim da re-zer-vi-shem spa-va-ći va-gon za no-ćni voz.*)

914. What's the schedule for the next ferry to the island?
Какав је распоред за следећи трајект до острва?
(*Ka-kav ye ras-po-red za sle-de-ći tra-jekt do ostr-va?*)

915. Are there any available seats on the evening bus to the beach?
Да ли има слободних места на вечерњем аутобусу за плажу?
(*Da li i-ma slo-bo-dnih me-sta na ve-cher-njem au-to-bu-su za pla-zhu?*)

916. Can I pay for my metro ticket with a mobile app?
Да ли могу да платим карту за метро преко мобилне апликације?
(*Da li mo-gu da pla-tim kar-tu za me-tro pre-ko mo-bil-ne a-pli-ka-tsi-je?*)

917. Is there a discount for purchasing tickets online?
Постоји ли попуст за куповину карата преко интернета?
(*Po-sto-ji li po-pust za ku-po-vi-nu ka-ra-ta pre-ko in-ter-ne-ta?*)

918. How much is the parking fee at the train station?
Колика је такса за паркирање на железничкој станици?
(*Ko-li-ka ye tak-sa za par-ki-ra-nje na že-lez-nič-koj sta-ni-tsi?*)

919. I'd like to reserve two seats for the next shuttle bus.
Желим да резервишем два места за следећи шатл аутобус.
(*Zhe-lim da re-zer-vi-shem dva me-sta za sle-de-ći shatl au-to-bus.*)

920. Do I need to validate my ticket before boarding the tram?
Да ли треба да валидирам карту пре уласка у трамвај?
(*Da li tre-ba da va-li-di-ram kar-tu pre u-las-ka u tram-vaj?*)

921. Can I buy a monthly pass for the subway?
Могу ли да купим месечну карту за метро?
(*Mo-gu li da ku-pim me-seč-nu kar-tu za me-tro?*)

922.   Are there any group rates for the boat tour?
Постоје ли групне цене за обилазак бродом?
(*Po-sto-je li gru-pne tse-ne za o-bi-lazak bro-dom?*)

> **Travel Story:** At a vineyard in the Šumadija region, a winemaker referred to his wine as, "Вино са душом," meaning "Wine with a soul."

Arranging Travel

923.   I need to book a flight to Paris for next week.
Треба да резервишем лет за Париз за следећу недељу.
(*Tre-ba da re-zer-vi-shem let za Pa-riz za sle-de-ću ne-de-lyu.*)

924.   What's the earliest departure time for the high-speed train?
Које је најраније време поласка брзог воза?
(*Ko-ye ye nai-ra-ni-ye vre-me po-las-ka br-zog vo-za?*)

925.   Can I change my bus ticket to a later time?
Могу ли да променим аутобуску карту за каснији термин?
(*Mo-gu li da pro-me-nim au-to-bu-sku kar-tu za kas-ni-ji ter-min?*)

926.   I'd like to rent a car for a week.
Желим да изнајмим аутомобил на недељу дана.
(*Že-lim da iz-naj-mim au-to-mo-bil na ne-de-lyu da-na.*)

927. Is there a direct flight to New York from here?
Да ли постоји директан лет за Њујорк одавде?
(*Da li po-sto-ji di-rek-tan let za Nju-jork o-da-vde?*)

928. I need to cancel my reservation for the cruise.
Треба да откажем резервацију за крстарење.
(*Tre-ba da ot-ka-žem re-zer-va-tsi-ju za krs-ta-re-nje.*)

929. Can you help me find a reliable taxi service for airport transfers?
Можете ли ми помоћи да пронађем поуздану такси услугу за трансфер до аеродрома?
(*Mo-že-te li mi po-mo-ći da pro-na-đem pou-zda-nu tak-si u-slu-gu za trans-fer do ae-ro-dro-ma?*)

930. I'm interested in a guided tour of the city. How can I arrange that?
Заинтересован сам за вођену туру по граду. Како то могу организовати?
(*Za-in-te-re-so-van sam za vo-đe-nu tu-ru po gra-du. Ka-ko to mo-gu or-ga-ni-zo-va-ti?*)

931. Do you have any information on overnight buses to the capital?
Имате ли информације о ноћним аутобусима за главни град?
(*I-ma-te li in-for-ma-tsi-je o noć-nim au-to-bu-si-ma za glav-ni grad?*)

932. I'd like to purchase a travel insurance policy for my trip.
Желим да купим путно осигурање за моје путовање.
(*Že-lim da ku-pim put-no o-si-gu-ra-nje za mo-je pu-to-va-nje.*)

933. Can you recommend a good travel agency for vacation packages?
Можете ли да препоручите добру туристичку агенцију за пакете одмора?
(*Mo-zhe-te li da pre-po-ru-chi-te do-bru too-ree-steech-koo a-gen-tsi-yu za pa-ke-te od-mo-ra?*)

934. I need a seat on the evening ferry to the island.
Потребно ми је место на вечерњем броду за острво.
(*Po-treb-no mi ye me-sto na ve-che-rnyem bro-du za os-trvo.*)

935. How can I check the departure times for international flights?
Како могу да проверим времена поласка међународних летова?
(*Ka-ko mo-gu da pro-ve-rim vre-me-na po-las-ka med-yoo-na-rod-nih le-to-va?*)

936. Is there a shuttle service from the hotel to the train station?
Да ли постоји шатл сервис од хотела до железничке станице?
(*Da li po-sto-ji sha-tl ser-vis od ho-te-la do že-lez-nich-ke sta-ni-tse?*)

937. I'd like to charter a private boat for a day trip.
Желим да изнајмим приватни брод за дневни излет.
(*Že-lim da iz-nai-mim pri-vat-ni brod za dnev-ni iz-let.*)

938. Can you assist me in booking a vacation rental apartment?
Можете ли да ми помогнете у резервацији апартмана за изнајмљивање током одмора?
(*Mo-zhe-te li da mi po-mog-ne-te u re-zer-va-tsi-ji a-part-ma-na za iz-nai-mlyi-va-nje to-kom od-mo-ra?*)

939.   I need to arrange transportation for a group of 20 people.
       Треба да организујем транспорт за групу од 20 особа.
       (*Tre-ba da or-ga-ni-zu-jem trans-port za gru-pu od dva-de-set
       o-so-ba.*)

940.   What's the best way to get from the airport to the city center?
       **Који је најбољи начин да се дође од аеродрома до центра
       града?**
       (*Ko-ji ye nai-bo-lji na-chin da se do-đe od ae-ro-dro-ma do
       tsehn-tra gra-da?*)

941.   Can you help me find a pet-friendly accommodation option?
       **Можете ли да ми помогнете да нађем смештај прилагођен
       кућним љубимцима?**
       (*Mo-zhe-te li da mi po-mog-ne-te da na-đem sme-shtai
       pri-la-go-đen kooć-nim lju-bim-tsi-ma?*)

942.   I'd like to plan a road trip itinerary for a scenic drive.
       **Желим да планирам путнички маршрут за вожњу кроз
       пејзаже.**
       (*Že-lim da pla-ni-ram put-nich-ki marsh-rut za vozh-nju kroz
       pei-za-zhe.*)

> "Боље спречити него лечити."
> **"Better to prevent than to cure."**
> *It's better to avoid problems than to fix them.*

Word Search Puzzle: Transport & Directions

CAR
АУТОМОБИЛ
BUS
АУТОБУС
AIRPORT
АЕРОДРОМ
SUBWAY
МЕТРО
TAXI
ТАКСИ
STREET
УЛИЦА
MAP
МАПА
DIRECTION
СМЕР
TRAFFIC
САОБРАЋАЈ
PARKING
ПАРКИРАЊЕ
PEDESTRIAN
ПЕШАК
HIGHWAY
АУТОПУТ
BRIDGE
МОСТ
TICKET
КАРТА

```
M O W N D S O G X M Q T B P K
H A W K I U L N M B O L K Q U
Y С П L R B B M D M G J Q A O
D D N A E W E G D I R В Ц O T
I V C U C A I X A T W И T P S
M R V F T Y L U T X Л J H N U
J W J H I L P C E У X R A C B
Q A T A O K У X E K K J S G H
Л Z Ђ C N Б A I R P O R T N I
R И S A O П H N T K R Q E I G
Y R Б T P M E R S W R B K K H
A B У O G Б J Ш X E A G C R W
F A U B M T O N A D S J I A A
P G E J B O Q A P K C G T P Y
R I N R V X T G C A E D V G U
U W Y H Y N V Y W Њ P N I C Z
Q V Y H X J H I A U B G Y U K
A C P Z M Q U P M O T F M L L
И X F G S K И W C F E O K C S
A C I G Y K M A P C V M O S X
J E K H P N A N M G U T B A B
Y G P A A У H E C I F F A R T
I W П O T F P U K A T I Q S
G P V O Д R D H Y T B W M O E
G B П H P P J У P V S E A H F
J У Z O Z Y O A P A T M У F K
T C C B A J K M T P W B L L V
J A B P L Z B D O O N K I N A
P E D E S T R I A N H S G L F
Z H O Z T A I T B J P U V R B
```

Correct Answers:

SPECIAL OCCASIONS

- EXPRESSING WELL WISHES AND CONGRATULATIONS -
- CELEBRATIONS AND CULTURAL EVENTS -
- GIVING AND RECEIVING GIFTS -

Expressing Well Wishes & Congratulations

943. Congratulations on your graduation!
Честито дипломирање!
(Ches-tee-to dee-plo-mee-ra-nje!)

944. Best wishes for a long and happy marriage.
Најбоље жеље за дуг и срећан брак.
(Nai-bo-lje zhe-lje za doog ee sre-chan brak.)

945. Happy anniversary to a wonderful couple.
Срећна годишњица дивном пару.
(Srech-na go-deesh-nee-tsa dee-vnom pa-ru.)

946. Wishing you a speedy recovery.
Желим вам брз опоравак.
(Zhe-lim vam brz o-po-ra-vak.)

947. Congratulations on your new job!
Честито на новом посао!
(Ches-tee-to na no-vom po-sao!)

> **Travel Story:** During a visit to the Museum of Yugoslav History, a guide used the phrase, "Прошлост која обликује," meaning "The past that shapes."

948. May your retirement be filled with joy and relaxation.
Нека ваша пензија буде испуњена радошћу и опуштањем.
(Ne-ka va-sha pen-zi-ja bu-de ees-poo-nye-na ra-dosh-chu ee o-poo-shta-nyem.)

949. Best wishes on your engagement.
Најбоље жеље за веридбу.
(*Nai-bo-lje zhe-lje za ve-rid-bu.*)

950. Happy birthday! Have an amazing day.
Срећан рођендан! Имате невероватан дан.
(*Sre-chan rodh-dan! Ee-ma-te ne-ve-ro-va-tan dan.*)

> **Cultural Insight:** Serbians are proud of their Cyrillic alphabet, which is one of the official alphabets in Serbia.

951. Wishing you success in your new venture.
Желим вам успех у новом подухвату.
(*Zhe-lim vam us-peh oo no-vom po-doo-hva-tu.*)

952. Congratulations on your promotion!
Честито на унапређењу!
(*Ches-tee-to na oo-nap-re-dye-njoo!*)

953. Good luck on your exam—you've got this!
Срећно на испиту - имате ово!
(*Sre-chno na ees-pi-tu - ee-ma-te o-vo!*)

954. Best wishes for a safe journey.
Најбоље жеље за сигурно путовање.
(*Nai-bo-lje zhe-lje za see-goor-no poo-to-va-nje.*)

955. Happy retirement! Enjoy your newfound freedom.
Срећан пензионисање! Уживајте у новостеченој слободи.
(*Sre-chan pen-zi-o-nee-sa-nje! Oo-zhi-vai-te oo no-vo-ste-che-noi slo-bo-dee.*)

956. Congratulations on your new home.
      Честито на новом дому.
      (*Ches-tee-to na no-vom do-mu.*)

957. Wishing you a lifetime of love and happiness.
      Желим вам љубав и срећу током целог живота.
      (*Zhe-lim vam lyu-bav ee sre-chu to-kom tse-log zhi-vo-ta.*)

958. Best wishes on your upcoming wedding.
      Најбоље жеље за предстојеће венчање.
      (*Nai-bo-lje zhe-lje za pred-sto-yeh-che ven-cha-nye.*)

959. Congratulations on the arrival of your baby.
      Честито на доласку ваше бебе.
      (*Ches-tee-to na do-las-ku va-she be-be.*)

960. Sending you warmest thoughts and prayers.
      Шаљем вам најтоплије мисли и молитве.
      (*Shal-yem vam nai-top-lee-ye mis-li ee mo-lit-ve.*)

961. Happy holidays and a joyful New Year!
      Срећни празници и радосна Нова Година!
      (*Srech-nee praz-ni-tsi ee ra-dos-na No-va Go-dee-na!*)

962. Wishing you a wonderful and prosperous future.
      Желим вам дивну и просперитетну будућност.
      (*Zhe-lim vam div-nu ee pros-pe-ri-tet-nu bu-dooch-nost.*)

> **Idiomatic Expression:** "Јести као мрав." -
> Meaning: "To eat a lot."
> (Literal translation: "To eat like an ant.")

Celebrations & Cultural Events

963. I'm excited to attend the festival this weekend.
      Узбуђен сам због доласка на фестивал овог викенда.
      *(Uz-boo-dye-n sam zbo-g do-las-ka na fes-ti-val o-vog
      vee-ken-da.)*

964. Let's celebrate this special occasion together.
      Хајде да заједно прославимо овај посебан догађај.
      (Haj-de da za-yed-no pro-sla-vee-mo o-vai po-se-ban do-ga-djai.)

> **Fun Fact:** The Palić Film Festival is an important event
> in the Serbian film industry.

965. The cultural parade was a vibrant and colorful experience.
      Културна парада је била живописно искуство.
      (Kul-tur-na pa-ra-da ye bee-la zhi-vo-pis-no is-kus-tvo.)

966. I look forward to the annual family reunion.
      Са нетрпљењем ишчекујем годишње окупљање породице.
      *(Sa ne-trplye-nyem eesh-che-koo-yem go-dee-sh-nye
      o-ku-plya-nye po-ro-di-tse.)*

967. The fireworks display at the carnival was spectacular.
      Ватромет на карневалу је био спектакуларан.
      (Va-tro-met na kar-ne-va-lu ye bee-o spek-ta-ku-la-ran.)

968. It's always a blast at the neighborhood block party.
      Увек је забавно на комшијској блок забави.
      (U-vek ye za-bav-no na kom-shee-y-skoj blok za-ba-vee.)

969. Attending the local cultural fair is a tradition.
Посета локалног културног сајма је традиција.
(*Po-se-ta lo-kal-nog kul-tur-nog saj-ma ye tra-di-tsi-ya.*)

970. I'm thrilled to be part of the community celebration.
Одушевљен сам што сам део заједничке прославе.
(*O-dush-ev-ljen sam shto sam deo zaj-ed-nich-ke pro-sla-ve.*)

971. The music and dancing at the wedding were fantastic.
Музика и плес на венчању су били фантастични.
(*Mu-zi-ka ee ples na ven-cha-nju su bee-li fan-tas-tich-ni.*)

972. Let's join the festivities at the holiday parade.
Придружимо се свечаностима на празничној паради.
(*Prid-ru-zhi-mo se sve-cha-nos-ti-ma na praz-nich-noj pa-ra-di.*)

973. The cultural exchange event was enlightening.
Догађај културне размене био је просветљујући.
(*Do-ga-djaj kul-tur-ne raz-me-ne bee-o ye pro-svet-lju-ju-chi.*)

974. The food at the international festival was delicious.
Храна на међународном фестивалу је била укусна.
(*Hra-na na med-ju-na-rod-nom fes-ti-va-lu ye bee-la oo-kus-na.*)

Travel Story: On a rafting trip on the Drina River, a participant exclaimed, "Авантура живота," which translates to "Adventure of a lifetime."

975.   I had a great time at the costume party.
Одлично сам се провео/провела на маскенбалу.
(Od-lich-no sam se pro-ve-o/pro-ve-la na mas-ken-ba-lu.)

976.   Let's toast to a memorable evening!
Наздравље за незаборавно вече!
(Naz-dra-vlye za ne-za-bo-rav-no ve-che!)

977.   The concert was a musical extravaganza.
Концерт је био музички спектакл.
(Kon-cert ye bee-o mu-zich-ki spek-ta-kl.)

978.   I'm looking forward to the art exhibition.
Са нетрпљењем ишчекујем изложбу уметности.
(Sa ne-trplye-nyem eesh-che-ku-yem iz-lozh-bu oo-me-tos-ti.)

979.   The theater performance was outstanding.
Представа у позоришту је била изузетна.
(Pred-sta-va oo po-zo-rish-tu ye bee-la ee-zu-zet-na.)

980.   We should participate in the charity fundraiser.
Требало би да учествујемо у хуманитарној акцији.
(Tre-ba-lo bee da uch-stvo-ju-ye-mo oo hu-ma-ni-tar-noj ak-tsi-ji.)

981.   The sports tournament was thrilling to watch.
Гледање спортског турнира је било узбудљиво.
(Gle-dan-ye sports-kog tur-ni-ra ye bee-lo ooz-boo-dli-vo.)

982.   Let's embrace the local customs and traditions.
Прихватимо локалне обичаје и традиције.
(Pree-kha-ti-mo lo-kal-ne o-bi-chai-ye ee tra-di-tsi-ye.)

Giving and Receiving Gifts

983.   I hope you like this gift I got for you.
    **Надам се да ти се свиђа овај поклон који сам ти купио/
    купила.**
    *(Na-dam se da ti se svi-dja o-vaj pok-lon ko-ji sam ti
    ku-pio/ku-pi-la.)*

984.   Thank you for the thoughtful present!
    Хвала за пажљиви поклон!
    (Hva-la za pazh-lji-vi pok-lon!)

985.   It's a token of my appreciation.
    Ово је знак мог поштовања.
    (O-vo je znak mog posh-to-va-nja.)

986.   Here's a little something to brighten your day.
    Ево нешто мало да ти улепша дан.
    (E-vo neshto ma-lo da ti u-lep-sha dan.)

987.   I brought you a souvenir from my trip.
    Донео/ла сам ти сувенир са путовања.
    (Do-ne-o/la sam ti su-ve-nir sa pu-to-va-nja.)

988.   This gift is for you on your special day.
    Овај поклон је за тебе за твој посебан дан.
    (O-vaj pok-lon je za te-be za tvoj po-se-ban dan.)

989.   I got this with you in mind.
    Купио/ла сам ово мислећи на тебе.
    (Ku-pi-o/la sam o-vo mis-le-chi na te-be.)

990. You shouldn't have, but I love it!
Није требало, али ми се много свиђа!
(*Ni-je tre-ba-lo, a-li mi se mnogo svi-dja!*)

991. It's a small gesture of my gratitude.
Ово је мали гест моје захвалности.
(*O-vo je ma-li gest mo-je zah-va-lnos-ti.*)

992. I wanted to give you a little surprise.
Желео/ла сам да ти приредим мало изненађење.
(*Zhe-le-o/la sam da ti pri-re-dim ma-lo iz-ne-na-dje-nje.*)

993. I hope this gift brings you joy.
Надам се да ће ти овај поклон донети радост.
(*Na-dam se da che ti o-vaj pok-lon do-ne-ti ra-dost.*)

994. It's a symbol of our friendship.
Ово је симбол нашег пријатељства.
(*O-vo je sim-bol na-sheg pri-ja-telj-stva.*)

995. This is just a token of my love.
Ово је само знак моје љубави.
(*O-vo je sa-mo znak mo-je lju-ba-vi.*)

996. I knew you'd appreciate this.
Знао/ла сам да ћеш ово ценити.
(*Zna-o/la sam da chesh o-vo ce-ni-ti.*)

997. I wanted to spoil you a bit.
Желео/ла сам мало да те размазим.
(*Zhe-le-o/la sam ma-lo da te raz-ma-zim.*)

998. This gift is for your hard work.
Овај поклон је за твој труд.
(*O-vaj pok-lon je za tvoj trud.*)

999. I hope you find this useful.
Надам се да ће ти ово бити корисно.
(*Na-dam se da će ti o-vo bi-ti ko-ris-no.*)

1000. It's a sign of my affection.
Ово је знак моје наклоности.
(*O-vo je znak mo-je nak-lo-nos-ti.*)

1001. I brought you a little memento.
Донео/ла сам ти малу успомену.
(*Do-ne-o/la sam ti ma-lu us-po-me-nu.*)

"Упорност се исплати."
"Persistence pays off."
Steady effort leads to success.

Interactive Challenge: Special Occasions
(Link each English word with their corresponding meaning in Serbian)

1) Celebration	Наздравље
2) Gift	Дипломирање
3) Party	Журка
4) Anniversary	Рођендан
5) Congratulations	Венчање
6) Wedding	Честитке
7) Birthday	Изненађење
8) Graduation	Поклон
9) Holiday	Празник
10) Ceremony	Церемонија
11) Tradition	Прослава
12) Festive	Годишњица
13) Greeting	Свечан
14) Toast	Традиција
15) Surprise	Поздрав

Correct Answers:

1. Celebration - Прослава
2. Gift - Поклон
3. Party - Журка
4. Anniversary - Годишњица
5. Congratulations - Честитке
6. Wedding - Венчање
7. Birthday - Рођендан
8. Graduation - Дипломирање
9. Holiday - Празник
10. Ceremony - Церемонија
11. Tradition - Традиција
12. Festive - Свечан
13. Greeting - Поздрав
14. Toast - Наздравље
15. Surprise - Изненађење

CONCLUSION

Congratulations on reaching the conclusion of "The Ultimate Serbian Phrase Book." As you embark on your journey through the diverse and rich landscapes of Serbia, from the vibrant streets of Belgrade to the tranquil beauty of the Danube River, your dedication to learning Serbian is commendable.

This phrasebook has been a steadfast companion, offering crucial phrases and expressions to enhance your communication seamlessly. You've navigated from basic greetings like "Здраво" (Zdravo) and "Добро вече" (Dobro veče) to more complex expressions, preparing yourself for varied interactions, immersive experiences, and a deeper appreciation of Serbia's cultural tapestry.

Learning a language is more than acquiring a skill; it's about connecting with the soul of a culture. Your commitment has built a solid foundation for fluency in Serbian.

If this phrasebook has contributed to your language learning journey, I would be thrilled to hear about it! You can connect with me on Instagram: **@adriangruszka**. Share your adventures, seek advice, or simply say "Здраво!" I'd be overjoyed if you mention this book on social media and tag me – I'm eager to celebrate your strides in mastering Serbian.

For more resources, deeper insights, and updates, please visit **www.adriangee.com**. There, you'll discover a treasure trove of information, including recommended courses and a community of fellow language enthusiasts ready to support your ongoing educational journey.

Embracing a new language opens the door to new relationships and perspectives. Your passion for learning and adapting is your most significant asset in this linguistic adventure. Embrace every chance to learn, interact, and deepen your understanding of Serbian culture and way of life.

Срећно! (Good luck!) Continue to practice with dedication, refine your skills, and most importantly, enjoy each step of your Serbian language journey.

Хвала вам много! (Thank you very much!) for choosing this phrasebook. May your future explorations be filled with enriching conversations and achievements as you dive deeper into the captivating world of languages!

- Adrian Gee

.

Made in the USA
Coppell, TX
21 January 2025

44778834R00142